Prolegomena to the Study of the Second Jewish Revolt (A.D. 132-135)

Shimon Applebaum

BAR Supplementary Series 7
1976

British Archaeological Reports

122 Banbury Road, Oxford OX2 7BP, England

GENERAL EDITORS

A.C.C. Brodribb, M.A.　　　　　　　A.R. Hands, B.Sc., M.A., D.Phil.
Mrs. Y.M. Hands　　　　　　　　　　D.R. Walker, M.A.

B.A.R. Supplementary Series 7, 1976: "Prolegomena to the Study of the Second Jewish Revolt".
© Shimon Applebaum, 1976.

The author's moral rights under the 1988 UK Copyright, Designs and Patents Act are hereby expressly asserted.

All rights reserved. No part of this work may be copied, reproduced, stored, sold, distributed, scanned, saved in any form of digital format or transmitted in any form digitally, without the written permission of the Publisher.

ISBN 9780904531398 paperback
ISBN 9781407351285 e-book
DOI https://doi.org/10.30861/9780904531398
A catalogue record for this book is available from the British Library

This book is available at www.barpublishing.com

CONTENTS

	Page
ACKNOWLEDGEMENTS	
PRINCIPAL ABBREVIATIONS	
FOREWARD	1
The Political Background	2
Immediate Causes	5
The Economic Situation	9
The Rural Tradition	15
Prior Unrest	17
The Geographical Scope of the Rising	22
Military Considerations	25
The Tactical Factors	35
The Contemporary Tactical Situation in the Roman Army	40
The Tactical Composition of the Roman Forces in Judaea	44
Judaea and Wales: a Comparison	49
The Final Phase	52
Gentile Participation?	56
Ben Kosba as Military Leader	58
CONCLUSIONS	63
APPENDIX:	
Roman Auxiliary Units which served, or probably served, in Hadrian's Jewish War	65
FOOTNOTES	69
MAPS:	
1. Judaea: The localities referred to in the text	99
2. Wales: Roman forts held in the year A.D. 110 and their relation to areas of native settlement	100

ACKNOWLEDGEMENTS

I am indebted to Colonel Ele'azar Galili for his critical reading of the first fifty pages of this work; various factors unfortunately prevented him from reading the whole. Professor Shemuel Safrai also read the text and saved me from a number of inaccuracies in the talmudic references. I am likewise grateful to my colleague Binyamin Izaak for various suggestions and corrections.

I further wish to record my thanks to the following colleagues, with whom I have discussed individual points or who have furnished me with information: Dr. Y. Algabish, Dr. B. Bar Kokhba (no relative of the Jewish commander), M. Ben Dov, Professor Eric Birley, Dr. D. Baatz, Gamliel Douer (Dept. of Forestry of the State of Israel), Dr. Gid'eon Förster, Professor M. Gihon, Dr. Yisrael Roll, Dr. M. Gil, the late Dr. L. Kadman, A. Kindler, (Dept. of Numismatics, the Museum ha-Aretz, Tel Aviv), Dr. M. Kokhvi, Professor B. Mazar, Dr. A 'Ovadiah, P. Porat, Professor A. L. Rivet, Dr. Graham Webster, Dr. R. P. Wright and Professor Y. Yadin. But for the views expressed here the responsibility is my own.

The leisure to write the present monograph I enjoyed in the course of a generous visiting fellowship granted by All Souls College, Oxford.

I finally wish to express my appreciation of the assistance rendered by the conscientious and hardworking staffs of the libraries of the University of Tel Aviv and the Ashmolean Museum, Oxford.

I also thank the School of Jewish Studies, University of Tel Aviv, who paid for the maps.

S. A.
February, 1976

PRINCIPAL ABBREVIATIONS

AA	Archäologische Anzeiger - Beiblatt zum Jahrbuch des Deutschen Archäologischen Instituts.
AASOR	Annual of the American School of Oriental Research.
AE	L'année epigraphique - Supplément de Revue archéologique.
AJA	American Journal of Archaeology.
ASAA	Annuario della Scuola archeologica di Atene.
BASOR	Bulletin of the American School of Oriental Research.
BGU	Ägyptische Urkunden aus den Staatlichen Museum zu Berlin.
BIES	Bulletin of the Israel Exploration Society (Heb. Yediot).
BRGK	Bericht der Römisch-Germanischen Kommission des Deutschen Archäologischen Instituts.
BSA	Annual of the British School at Athens.
CAH	Cambridge Ancient History.
CBA	A publication of the Council for British Archaeology.
CIA	Corpus Inscriptionum Atticarum.
CIG	Corpus Inscriptionum Graecarum.
CIL	Corpus Inscriptionum Latinarum.
CIJ	J.-B. Frey. Corpus Inscriptionum Iudaicarum, I, II, 1936-1952.
CPJ	Tcherikover, Fuks, Corpus Papyrorum Judaicarum, I-III, 1957-1964.
CRAI	Comptes-rendues de l'académie des inscriptions et belles-lettres.
DJD	Milik et al. Discoveries in the Judaean Desert.
GJV	E. Schürer, Geschichte des Jüdischen Volkes im Zeitalter Jesu Christi. I-III, 1901-1909.
HE	Historia Ecclesiae (Eusebius).
HTR	Harvard Theological Review.
IEJ	Israel Exploration Journal.
ILS	Inscriptiones Latinae Selectae. (H. Dessau).
JEA	Journal of Egyptian Archaeology.
JGAC	S. Applebaum, Jews and Greeks in Ancient Cyrene. 1969. (Heb.).
JHS	Journal of Hellenic Studies.
JQR	Jewish Quarterly Review.

JRS	Journal of Roman Studies.
Not. Dig.	Notitia Dignitatum utriusque Imperii. (ed. Seeck).
ORL	Fabricius *et al.* Der obergermanische-rätische Limes.
PBSR	Papers of the British School at Rome.
PEFQ	Palestine Exploration Fund Quarterly Statement.
PEQ	Palestine Exploration Quarterly.
PG	Cursus Patrologiae, Series Graeca (Migne).
Pjb	Palästina Jahrbuch.
PL	Cursus Patrologiae, Series Latina (Migne).
PW	Paully-Wissowa-Kroll, Realenzyklopädie der Classischen Altertumswissenschaft.
QDAP	Quarterly of the Department of Antiquities of the Government of Palestine.
RB	Revue biblique.
RétJ	Revue des études juives.
RIB	Collingwood, Wright, Roman Inscriptions in Britain, 1965.
SEG	Supplementum Epigraphicum Graecum.
SHA	Scriptores Historiae Augustae.
SHRE	M. Rostovtzeff, Social and Economic History of the Roman Empire, I, II, 1957.
ZDPV	Zeitschrift des Deutschen Palästinavereins.

ADDENDA and CORRIGENDA

Contents: for 'Foreward' read 'Foreword'
p. 21, l. 13: for 'mezuzal' read 'mezuzah'
      l. 38: for 'boleshot' read 'boleshet'
p. 27, l. 45: for 'consist' read 'consists'
p. 45, l. 38: for 'P.63' read 'P.65'
p. 56, l. 33: for 'Ghore' read 'Ghor'
p. 67, n. 26, l. 5: for 'vexxillationes' read 'vexillationes'
p. 85, n. 263a: for 'ex-centurion' read 'ex-decurion'
p. 88, n. 317: after l. 17 add: at full gallop.
p. 93, n. 400, l. 2: for ἐρηνωθῆναι read ἐρημωθῆναι

Map 1. Hippos should be □

    Neapolis: delete ⊙. ◇ should be ◆

    Naḥal Ḥever should be △

p. 98, Key. Hadrian, fortified should be ⊥⊥⊥⊥⊥⊥⊥⊥

Map 2 (Wales)

4.	Abergavenny	21.	Forden Gaer
6.	Brecon Gaer	22.	Gelligaer
7.	Bryn-y-Gefeiliau	23.	Leintwardine
8.	Caer Gai	26.	Llandovery
9.	Caerhun	27.	Llanio
10.	Caernarvon	30.	Pennal
12.	Caersws	34.	Tomen-y-Mur
14.	Carmarthen	35.	Trawscoed
15.	Castell Collen	36.	Usk

PROLEGOMENA TO THE STUDY OF THE SECOND JEWISH REVOLT
(AD 132-135)

FOREWORD

A recent reviewer in a prominent classical journal regretted the absence of a study of the social origins of the Second Jewish Revolt against Rome in the reign of Hadrian - the movement associated with the name of Shim'on ben Kosba. No adequate general work has been written on the rising, and if we exclude the evidence afforded in recent years by the discoveries in the Judaean Desert, Schürer's brief summary of the facts and sources (1901)[1] is still the most satisfactory that learning has to offer; this has now been brought up to date by Vermes' and Millar's reedition of Schürer's first volume.[2] In 1904 Adolph Buechler published a discussion of the problem of the theatre of the war and its limits in a paper which ranks almost alone in the literature produced after Schürer.[3] Among newer publications, S. Yeivin's War of Bar Kokhba (1946, second edition 1952) is useful for its account of Bethar and because it sets forth the talmudic and Samaritan sources bearing on the war, but as a historical survey it pays little attention to contemporary social and military evidence. Valuable as a subsequent historical account were the late Gedalyah Alon's chapters in his Hebrew History of the Jews of Eretz Yisrael in the Period of the Mishnah and the Talmud,[4] whose innovations were an essay on the constitution of the Jewish revolutionary commonwealth and the concentration of evidence for guerrilla activity in Judaea prior to the rebellion. In the archaeological field, The Discoveries at Wadi Murabba'at of Benoit, Milik and de Vaux (1961) opened a new era of knowledge and gave us the first contemporary documentary evidence on the rising in its later stages. S. Avramsky's Hebrew Bar Kokhba, Prince of Israel (1961) was a semi-popular work written immediately after the corresponding discoveries in the caverns of the Israel sector of the Judaean Desert. Yigael Yadin's Bar Kokhba (1971), is also a popular account of those discoveries, and the historical treatment, restricted to an appendix of sources, hardly added much. His first volume on the Nahal Hever finds, (Judaean Desert Studies, The Finds from the Bar Kokhba Period in the Cave of the Letters, 1963), is of course the detailed and competent professional volume which these finds deserve, but the full account of the material from the other sites then explored is still to come.[5] In any case, the sensational character of the contents of the Judaean caves should not be allowed to impair the historian's sense of proportion; they throw a dramatic light on the last tragic phases of the Jewish resistance, and obliquely upon some of its previous stages, but they add comparatively little to our knowledge of the causes and course of the war. Lucette Huteau-Dubois' "Les sursauts du nationalisme juif contre l'occupation Romaine de Massada à Bar Kokhba" (RétJ 127, 1968, pp. 133 sqq.) deals with the revolt of 132-135 in her later sections. Her study takes no account of geographical or archaeological data (excepting the Judaean Desert documents), and is unfortunately insufficiently furnished with references. Shortly after the Naḥal Ḥever discoveries, the late Y. Devir produced a spirited and poetic book which argued the connection of Ben Kosba with the Qumran sect;[6] quite irrespective of the validity of his ideas, he was the first thinker to attempt the restoration of the mystical and ideological world of the revolt, and to relate it to talmudic sources.

Productive of progress on the historical side has been the recent work of the numismatists; Mildenberg, Kadman, Meshorer and Kindler[7] have done much to ascertain the geographical extent of the revolt, its centres and its progress. Of importance also have been the Judaean Wilderness archaeological surveys conducted in the years 1967 and 1968 by the Society for the Archaeological Survey of Israel.[8] These have found a vast variety of Roman and other installations in the desert (most of which await published analysis) and added important Roman military sites in the vicinity of Bethar and in the Teqoa'-Ziph region. Some other recent publications will be referred to in the course of the present discussion.

THE POLITICAL BACKGROUND

What has not been attempted on any scale has been a study of the rising that combines attention to the situation in the Roman Empire as a whole and Hadrian's policy within it, with an adequate knowledge of Roman military developments and the Jewish aspect as restorable from talmudic and other Jewish sources. What follows cannot claim to fulfil all these requirements; it is an initial essay that may point the way to a fuller achievement.

* * *

However discordant an element the Jews may have constituted in the concert of Empire till the rebellion of 70, they composed a still harder core of bitter resentment after the destruction of the Temple. Their ferment was not, however, a ferment of simple resistance. Probably Judaism had never been so influential as a proselytizing faith as in the last decades of the 1st century AD. Under Domitian it looks very much as if among the Senatorial aristocracy judaization had become a form of protest against Domitian's terror.[9] The Emperor's assassination was the direct result of the penalization of Flavius Clemens and his wife Domitilla for judaization.[10] The affair may have had more extended ramifications among judaizers, and Jewish tradition records a contemporary chapter both of martyrdom among distinguished Roman proselytes and an alleged plan of the authorities to wipe out the Jewish nation.[11] Domitian was certainly nervous of the possibility of a renewed Jewish messianic movement; he investigated the kindred of Jesus as alleged descendants of David in Judaea; Trajan put some of them to death.[12] The Zealot opposition to tyranny was fresh in the minds of the Roman intellectuals: Epictetus cited them,[13] and he formed a link between high civil-servant circles and the Cynic opposition, whose leaders Domitian had found it expedient to banish. One of the senatorial victims of Domitian's prosecution, M' Acilius Glabrio, later executed for judaization, was forced by the Emperor to vanquish a lion in single combat;[14] this might be the true explanation of the man struggling with a lion pictured on an amulet found among the relics of Ben Kosba's followers in the Naḥal Ḥever cave.[15]

Whatever the case, Nerva's wide advertisement of the abolition of the abuses involved in Domitian's collection of the Jewish tax,[16] suggests that more than born Jews had been victimized, and that a wide public opinion had to be reconciliated. Tacitus' savage and slanderous misrepresentation of Jewish history and character,[17] all the more significant because it came from the pen of an aristocrat singularly well equipped to know that the facts were more complex,[18] shows that conservative Romans regarded the struggle with Judaism as still pending. However unjust Tacitus' allegations, his apprehension was justified. In 115 broke out the spectacular and murderous revolt of the Jewish Diaspora centres of Cyrene, Egypt and Cyprus.[19] This cannot be our subject here: suffice it to say that it reflected the results, not merely of a long period of conflict with Greek populations in those centres,[20] but a conviction that accounts must be settled with the pagan Empire once and for all. Messianic and Zealot trends were here equally mingled; links with the Qumran sectarian ideology are strongly suggested. The gravity of the movement is indicated by the official Roman term applied to it, namely, <u>tumultus</u>, a situation of emergency regarded as graver than normal war.[21]

In the present context, the importance of the <u>tumultus Iudaicus</u> is in its results; it created a certain attitude among Roman administrators in the next decades; it destroyed three of the most important Jewish communities of the Diaspora, producing a shift in the balance of power in the eastern Empire and the increased isolation of the community in Judaea. It was to cause Hadrian to lean more heavily on the Greek cities of that area. It probably doomed the revolt of 132 to failure in advance. It did not, thanks to its timing and its successful phase at the height of Trajan's second Parthian campaign, remove Roman apprehensions arising from the presence of large Jewish populations both sides of the eastern frontier.[22]

Nor were Hadrian's apprehensions calmed by his awareness that the eastern part of the Empire presented all the dangers of cultural heterogeneity and social-religious fragmentation.[23] The retreat to the Euphrates frontier and the giving up of Trajan's Parthian accessions made the consolidation of the eastern border-provinces, of which Syria was the core and Judaea an extension, all the more vital: the annexation of the Arabian province simplified the problem, providing a pied-à-terre east of the Judaean province. Hadrian's own hold on power in his initial years was to no small degree threatened by loss of prestige through his retreat from Parthia, and he could afford no immediate wars in that quarter, least of all hostilities that might bring dangerous commanders such as Lusius Quietus and Cornelius Palma to the fore.[24]

These last apprehensions had perhaps faded by the latter part of Hadrian's reign, but the east still needed an active policy. Rome had always preferred the Greek element as a consolidating factor in the eastern provinces;[25] in Egypt, while dividing the Greeks and Jews against each other (if that was needed) in order to rule, and maintaining a certain balance of privileges, the imperial government basically rated the Greeks higher for tax-exemption, and in any major clash between the two could be relied upon to favour them.[26] Rome's agent, Herod, had tipped the scales in favour of the Greeks in Judaea by his policy of urbanization and the situation was amply demonstrated in the year 66 by the intercommunal clashes in Caesarea and in almost every mixed hellenistic city of Judaea and Syria.[27] The annexation of Provincia Arabia came not only as the solution of an awkward administrative problem, namely, virtual Roman control of the important Decapolis cities of Transjordan which were nominally in Nabataea,[28] or as a means of seizing the important trade-routes from southern Arabia to Syria and across the Negev - but also as a means of cutting off Judaea from Parthia[29] and of obtaining potential military bases against an unreliable region to westward.

Hadrian's personal attitude to Jews and Judaism is unknown. The statement of the <u>Historia Augusta</u> that he disliked "foreign religions" is vague,[30] and certainly did not apply to the hellenistic cults. Nor did it apply, at least in political relations, to the oriental cults: he was not above inaugurating and handsomely endowing a Paneguris Hadriane in honour of the god Marnas at Gaza.[31] By education and inclination he was a hellenist, and may thus be classed with the hellenizing emperors Gaius and Nero - at least in one respect additional to his sympathy for things Greek - namely, in his lack of readiness to take the Jews as a factor to be compromised with where political decisions were concerned, unless considerable pressure was exerted upon him. This peculiar blind spot might have sufficed to produce grave results, but it may have been complicated by the political tradition which he had derived from his immediate predecessor. He had been Trajan's close associate before his own succession, and spent much time in his company. Trajan's own father had commanded the Tenth Legion in the Jewish war of 66-73,[32] and with it overrun much of the Jewish region east of Jordan. Syme is disposed to credit him with the military reorganization of the Syrian frontier.[33] The Emperor Trajan himself owed part of his failure against Parthia to the Jewish rising in his rear and in Mosopotamia, and had to expend no small effort in its suppression both sides of the frontier. At this juncture Hadrian was legate of Syria,[34] and was obliged to despatch forces to Cyprus in order to put down the Jewish insurgents in that island;[35] he certainly crossed to the island to oversee operations.[36] After Trajan's death he may well have found need to deal, albeit from a distance, with repercussions of the revolt in Syria, in the form of the activities of the Jews Pappus and Lulianus, who were running in "illegal immigrants" between Antioch and Ptolemais-'Akko - i.e. probably from Cyprus - and sending them to Jerusalem.[37] After the end of the revolt, Hadrian faced the practical and cultural problems involved in the rehabilitation of Egypt,[38] Cyrenaica[39] and Cyprus,[40] which had suffered gravely at the hands of the insurgents. At the outset of his reign, therefore, he would have acquired an abiding awareness of the Jews as a destructive and seditious group whose treasonable activities belonged to no one province and whose existence was not confined to the Empire.

Such an impression would surely have been sufficient to account for what amounted to a major policy decision taken by Hadrian at a later point in his reign: the decision to put an end to Judaism for good and all. In the meantime, he may have been undecided in his estimate of the forces and factors; such would appear to be the conclusion to be drawn from his programme for Jerusalem. At the very beginning of his rule, he seems to have planned to reestablish the city; so much is reported by a number of sources which,[41] despite their confused character and varying remoteness from the time concerned, are too numerous not to reflect some historical nucleus. Alon, after an analysis of these reports,[42] concluded that they represented a real move on the part of the Emperor to rebuild the town, but this design was misinterpreted by part of the Jewish population as an intention to renew the Temple cult. Whatever the case, the decision was rescinded and the project shelved. Nothing need here surprise us, but if the episode is historical, it teaches us that the project remained in Hadrian's mind, and it was to bear fruit at a later stage, when the military and political climate appeared to be more favourable to it.

On the whole we may venture to conclude that Hadrian's attitude to the Jews, in so far as indirect evidence is at our disposal, would have been a compound of the cultural strangeness intensified by his hellenist propensities, and a negative orientation derived from his association with Trajan, from his aristocratic Roman prejudices and from his conception of the problems inherent in Rome's control of the east. His soldierly qualities would have caused him to gauge the Jews as a military factor, and here his direct experience might have led him to overestimate the Jews of the Diaspora and to underestimate the Jews of Judaea.

IMMEDIATE CAUSES

As Hadrian's reign progressed, there was much in his intensive strengthening of the Greek communities which was bound to arouse Jewish apprehension. There is no need to dwell in detail on the enormous effort and capital invested by Hadrian in the cultural, physical and religious resuscitation of Greek life in the eastern provinces of the Empire.[43] His attachment to the Greek cults is especially emphasized by his initiation at Eleusis and by his completion of the Temple of Zeus Olympios in 130-132.[44] Some scholarly Athenians may have recalled that the Temple was originally conceived and begun by the tyrant Peisistratus, the slayers of whose son became the symbol of their city's liberty;[45] the Jews no doubt remembered that its continuer had been Antiochus Epiphanes, who possibly hung the veil of the Temple of Jerusalem in the Temple of Zeus at Olympia.[46] The recollection would have been driven home by Hadrian's act of self-deification on the inauguration of the shrine: he took the title "Olympios";[47] his statue stood with that of the Olympian within the building;[48] his altar with that of Zeus' before it.[49] Symbols of adulation and acknowledgements of his divinity poured in from the provinces; the interior of the naos was a forest of statues.[50] There were doubtless repercussions in the provinces themselves, and loyal imitative gestures.[51] The reverence was not purchased by self-deification alone, but also by the plethora of new buildings, cultic festivals and public amenities erected, often within a new organisational framework; the Panhellenic League, of Hadrian's devising, celebrated its first all-Greek festivity in 131/2.[52]

Hadrian's Syrian journey, as he moved from Asia to Egypt between 129 and 130, may have been a trifle less successful. Despite the shower of honours, cultural events and public amenities conferred by the Emperor on Antioch, Antiochenses inter haec ita odio habuit ut Syriam a Phoenice separare voluit ne tot civitatum metropolis Antiochia diceretur, says the Augustan History,[53] and at once goes on to refer to the Jewish rising. The first report is perhaps an exaggeration or a distortion   (see below, p. 57), but the linking of the two situations may be significant. Hadrian's arrival in Judaea was celebrated by coins ominously free of any allusion to the people who gave their name to the country.   "We have," notes Professor Jocelyn Toynbee, [54] "instead of a characteristic native Judaea, defeated by Roman arms, a Greek standing goddess, the Judaea of Hadrian's creation, sacrificing before Hadrian with her children."[55] The symbolism expressed the marked obsequiousness of its inhabitants. Dio's passage on Hadrian's negative features of character may read too much like the Augustan History[56] in its capsulated isolation from the rest of the account, but Hadrian's alleged inability to tolerate competitors in any field may have been a fact,[57] perhaps to be extended to explain his negative reaction to the only people in the Empire perverse enough to ignore his divinity. [57a]

There may have been much else that it was convenient to ignore: the southern desert was insecure, and the doubling of Judaea's garrison may have taken place several years before (see below, p. 19). One Jewish centre Hadrian may have visited, namely, Tiberias, erected by the astute Antipas as a Jewish city organized on the Greek model. It may not yet have been the pronounced centre of Jewish scholarship and social autonomy that it was to become in the later 2nd century, but it must nevertheless have been preponderantly Jewish. [58] Here Hadrian had set up, or now erected, a Hadrianeium in his own honour;[59] clearly whatever his notions of imperial tact, either he was relying on the pliancy, or obstinate indifference, of what was regarded as a hellenized Jewish citizenry, or he was not interested in being tactful. The statues before the Hadrianeium or some kindred edifice in the city were not hacked down till about a century later[60]- as good an indication as any that Tiberias had remained outside the dissident area in 132-135 (and care was taken even then to leave intact a statue known to have been the object of pagan reverence). Hadrian's visits to Petra, Caesarea Maritima and Gaza tell us little more, but it is now almost certain that to this tour belonged his decision to convert Jerusalem to Aelia Capitolina (see below, p. 8.) As Hadrian proceeded to Egypt, he turned aside to honour the tomb of Pompey near Pelusium, and gave orders for its restoration. [61] The Julio-Claudians in whose footsteps Hadrian trod had little cause to love Pompey, but it was doubtless as conqueror of the orient that Hadrian honoured him, and the mausoleum is likely enough to have suffered at the hands of the Jewish insurgents of 115-117. [62] The Jews, in their turn, must have noted the Emperor's ostentatious respect for the first Roman desecrator of their Temple. [63].

Nor was Hadrian's visit to Egypt devoid of incidents likely to provoke their sensitivity. The death of the imperial favourite Antinous was followed by the establishment of a memorial city in Egypt and a divine cult in his memory which spread throughout the eastern Empire. [64] Even among the aristocrats of a permissive age, criticism was subsequently implied or uttered;[65] for the Jews, this was the deification of homosexuality, and consultation of the Jewish Oracula Sibyllina, which tell us much of the critical Jewish attitude in this period, will show how bitterly this gentile transgression was denounced by the prophets of Divine vengeance and the anticipated messianic order. [66]

In short, a gigantic campaign devoted to the propagation, strengthening and glorification of idol-worship among the centres of the same Greek population that had been engaged in sanguinary conflict with the Jewries of the eastern Mediterranean for over two centuries, that had been resuscitated thanks to Pompey's destruction of the Hasmonean kingdom, and aided Titus to destroy the Temple - had culminated in the blasphemous self-deification of the ruler and the apotheosis of homosexuality. If any doubt had been entertained as to the final consequence of such a policy, it was dissipated by the decision to convert Jerusalem to Aelia Capitolina (it was to Jupiter Capitolinus at Rome that the Jewish tax had been paid since 70),[67] and by Hadrian's order prohibiting circumcision.[68]

Both orders have been the subject of long drawnout controversy, and a number of scholars have argued that they were the result, not the cause, of the Jewish rebellion of 132.

The evidence of talmudic literature is not absolutely decisive as to whether the prohibition to circumcise preceded the war, as the Historia Augusta states, but taken on the whole heavily favours the view that it did. Tos. Shab. XVI, 9 says that Jews who had endeavoured to efface their circumcision by operation must be circumcised. R. Judah objects that this is dangerous, and the recorded reply is: "Many were circumcised in Ben Kosba's time yet begot children and did not die." Alon[69] has pointed out that the prohibition of the rite would not necessarily have induced Jews to efface its results, such an act being simply the product of a desire to assimilate; the recircumcision enforced by Ben Kosba would have been part of the reimplementation of Judaism under an independent Jewish régime. Alon nevertheless concluded that such a policy implied that Hadrian's prohibition had been promulgated before the rising of 132. Another rabbinical passage bearing on the question is the reference of R. Ishmael ben Elisha'[70] to decrees against the performance of various Jewish commandments, including the seven-day celebration which preceded circumcision. As R. Ishmael died before the rebellion,[71] this would also imply that circumcision was banned before it broke out. Here again Alon expressed the opinion that R. Ishmael's words described a complete period beginning in 70, during which the Roman government had made the performance of the commandments more difficult, but nevertheless accepted the prior prohibition as historical. It should be added that the Mekhilta de-R. Ishmael[72] attributes to the same scholar the observation that "everything for which Israel gave her life she has been able to maintain, and all those things for which Israel has not given her life have not been maintained; the Sabbath, circumcision, study of the Law, and baptism - all these have been maintained; but the things for which Israel has not given her life - such as the Temple, freedom of jurisdiction, the seventh-year fallow and the jubilee year - have not been maintained." This statement is ascribed by Siphre Deuteronomy[73] to R. Simon ben Gamliel (active AD 140-165), and while the uncertain attribution favours the antiquity of the utterance, Mekhilta is the older document, and the already cited reference by R. Ishmael to the banning of circumcision might be taken to support his authorship in the present case.

Important as independent testimony is the Epistle of Barnabas, written after 70; it is stated therein (9:4) that circumcision has been prohibited, further that the prophecy of Isaiah (49:17) of the destruction of the Temple has been fulfilled, and that it will be rebuilt by Israel's enemies. Schürer supported a date of about 130 for the Epistle on the evidence of this last passage,[74] which is evidently a later interpolation. Smallwood[75] rejects the idea that the reference is to Hadrian's project for building a temple of Jupiter on the Temple site. As we have since learned that Aelia was begun before the outbreak of the Jewish war (see below), her objection now seems less cogent, and the Epistle may today be viewed as valid evidence for the prior banning of circumcision. All these considerations apart, however, one commonsense observation seems in place. If the prohibition was imposed after the revolt, it would be interpretable as a punishment. But the general nature of the decree (it remained applicable to non-Jews after Pius had rescinded it in respect of Jews)[76] surely implies that it was not a punishment, and therefore preceded the revolt.

The abolition of the rite as the first fundamental commandment devolving upon the Jew, meant, quite logically, the end of Judaism. That the order was the extension of a general enactment against castration, and applicable not only to Jews, cannot justify the decision; relevant is Anatole France's acid comment, that all men are equal before the law, which permits neither the rich man nor the poor to sleep on a bench in the park. In any case, Hadrian, as an educated man with expert advisers at his call, must have been aware of the difference between castration and circumcision, and it is hard to think that he did not know what the latter's abolition meant for the Jews.

Dio states[77] that the decision to found Aelia preceded the rising; Eusebius[78] attributes the act to the period succeeding the war. But Dio lived closer to events, and was free of Eusebius' theologically inspired motive to make Jewish sufferings and misfortunes the just punishment for their own transgressions. Today there is no longer much doubt that the building of Aelia had already begun before the Jewish war broke out. On this question new archaeological evidence is available, and its language is clear. Coin-hoards from the Hebron area now published by Meshorer possess a composition of which the following instance is typical: Trajan and Hadrian to the year 131 - 35 coins; Ben Kosba - 5 coins; Aelia Capitolina - one coin.[79] Four further hoards furnishing similar evidence and found in the same district, have now been published by Meshorer.[80] They include gold and silver coins of Ben Kosba in considerable numbers, also Roman bronze and silver provincial issues. They comprised the following groups: 1) Large silver sela'im of Ben Kosba, each valuing four denarii; 2) Silver denarii of Ben Kosba; 3) Bronze coins in three denominations (it is not stated if these are Roman or Jewish); 4) Roman provincial tetradrachms struck at Antioch and Tyre in the reigns of Nero, Otho, Galba, Vespasian, Titus, Domitian and Trajan; 5) Roman provincial denarii struck at Caesarea of Cappadocia and at Bostra; 6) Bronze coins of the cities of Judaea and its vicinity. All the coins of Ben Kosba are overstruck on Roman coins, none of which is later than the year 131, the latest being those of Hadrian of that year. All hoards contain Hadrianic issues struck at Aelia Capitolina.

It is therefore to be assumed that the decisions to prohibit circumcision and to found Aelia were taken in the same period if not at the same time, and that they involved a major change of policy on the part of the Emperor. Even after the rebellion of 70, Vespasian and Titus had refused to abolish the communal rights of the Jewish populations of Antioch and Alexandria.[81] Ironically enough, the tax paid by Jews to the Fiscus Iudaicus itself was a confirmation of the legality of Judaism.[82] Domitian seems to have victimized proselytization and concealment of Jewish identity, but at no point placed Judaism beyond the law, although a rabbinical tradition exists that he was planning to do so.[83] What Trajan intended to do after the Tumultus Iudaicus is unrecorded, but Hadrian would seem to have regarded the virtual extermination of the Jewish communities of Egypt, Cyrene and Cyprus as an adequate penalty at the time of his accession. In Syria nevertheless there are traces in talmudic tradition of actual religious persecution conducted by the Roman authority, in the form of an attempt - presumably by Lusius Quietus - to coerce Lulianus and Pappus into offering libations to the gods.[84] Hadrian's decision, therefore, was either an act of callous indifference based on a complete unawareness of the nature of Judaism and the reaction which such a policy was bound to produce (implying an absence of information and experienced advice), or he took a calculated risk, believing that resistance could be easily overcome. But it is hard to reconcile the taking of such a risk with Hadrian's much-travelled knowledge of his Empire, his manifold expertise in a variety of branches of knowledge, his farflung grasp of military frontier problems and his preparedness for humane and pliable measures of reform. It seems moreover clear, that however implemented, the anti-circumcision law applied, at least theoretically, to the entire Empire - as is indicated by the appearance of Hadrian's edicts on castration and Pius' on circumcision in the Digesta.[85] It meant the death of a people.

THE ECONOMIC SITUATION

The situation produced by the two imperial decisions of 130-131 would have been such as to warrant an explosion among Jewry. But it seems highly probable that Judaea had been in ferment for some years; the destruction of the Temple had been quite sufficient to create an economic and psychological situation ultimately productive of renewed violence.

In 1912 Adolph Buechler dealt in a thorough manner with the question of the economic situation in Judaea after 70.[85a] While he could demonstrate great poverty and suffering in the country, he also adduced a good deal of evidence for the existence of land owned by Jews,[86] and for its unrestricted transfer or leasing.[87] But most of these cases are in or about Lydda which, with Jamnia, (Yavneh), was a point where Jewish collaborators and moderates had been concentrated by Vespasian.[88] We are told that Vespasian founded no new cities in Judaea, but kept the χώρα for himself, κελεύων πᾶσαν γῆν ἀποδόσθαι τῶν Ἰουδαίων .[89] I think Schürer was almost certainly right when he solved the apparent contradiction between the first and second parts of this statement by interpreting ἀποδόσθαι as "to lease out" rather than as "give away" or "sell",[90] and although it is probable enough that confiscations were confined mainly to the lands of insurgents, there was doubtless a very considerable growth of imperial domain land in the country.[91] Possible evidence that confiscated lands in Judaea were in the main retained by the fiscus rather than sold up is M. Gittin V, 6, which reads: "There was no Siqariqon in Judaea in respect of those killed in the war, [but] from that time onward the Siqariqon applied." Jer. Gittin V, 6 adds: "In Galilee the Siqariqon has always applied." Siqariqon refers to regulations made by the scholars restricting the right of Jews to acquire property confiscated from other Jews by the Roman government as the result of the wars of 66-73 and 132-135. The discussion here concerns the intermediate period; as the reason for the non-application of these restrictions in Judaea, Tos. Gittin V, 47 adds: "for the sake of the resettlement of the country", i.e. to renew and to perpetuate its Jewish population. This means, that losses of Jewish inhabitants and lands there had been heavier than in Galilee, and hence no obstacles were placed before the reacquisition of property by survivors; but it does not necessarily mean that more land was being sold on the market; just the opposite might well have been the case, and if it was, there would be grounds for supposing that the accretion of crown-lands in Judaea might have been considerable.

The most interesting problem in this context is the interpretation of the testimony offered by talmudic sources on the tenurial situation in this period. This centres on the appearance of a class of landholder known in Hebrew as the matziqim; sometimes the term is interchanged with the word anasim. On the assumption that both words are Hebrew in origin, matziq would mean one who harasses; anas a violator, one who gains his ends by violence.[92]

The clearest characterization of the matziqim is to be found in two midrashim, Midrash Siphri de-Bei Rav (Friedmann, paras, 317, 357), on Deuteronomy, and Midrash Tannaim (Hoffman, pp. 198, 317) on the same book. The two commentaries possess some passages in common; the first is credited to the house of Rabbi (Judah the Prince), whose floruit was in the last decades of the 2nd century; the second to the scholars whose rulings were embodied in the Mishnah, redacted under Judah. The manuscripts are very corrupt, but evidently contain some material not later than the 2nd century, as will be clear from a scrutiny of the two passages relevant to our theme.[92a] It should be noted that much of these texts consists of critical comment, frequently satirical, on current affairs, masquerading as interpretation - a particularly Jewish genre of the period,[93] later adopted also, for instance, by Jerome.

Both books reproduce, as comment on Deut. 34:1, complete lists of the regions of the country which are being "bullied" by the matziqim.[94] Siphri de-Bei Rav[95] then proceeds: "And he shall eat the increase of my fields - these are the kingdoms (i.e. the Roman Empire); and he made them to suck honey out of the rock - these are the matziqim who have taken hold of the Land of Israel and it is as hard to keep from them a farthing (because they are are as hard) as rock, and tomorrow Israel inherits their property which is as sweet to them as honey and oil." Midrash Tannaim[96] continues the same text: "Butter of kine - these are their consuls and their prefects (hegemonim); with milk of sheep - these are their cleruchs; and rams - these are their beneficarii; of the breed of Bashan - these are their centurions who collect money from both of them; and goats - these are their senators; with the milk of roast wheat ears - these are their highborn ladies (matroniot)."

It is clear from the above passages that the matziqim were men who had seized Jewish landed property and either expelled the original owners ("and they have taken hold of Israel and driven them from their homes..."),[97] or are levying continual exactions from them ("it is as hard to keep from them a farthing" etc.). They are present in almost every part of the country from Galilee to the Darom (the south-west of Judaea bordering on the Negev); the mention of their presence at Tzoar, at the south end of the Dead Sea, if it may be taken seriously, would indicate that the list is not prior to Trajan's annexation of Nabataea (A.D. 106/7). The association of the matziqim with the Roman administration is also evident: "they are balashim who have become associated (בללו) with the government and will go to hell with it."[97a] A boleshet, according to an anecdote in Tosefta in which R. Simon of Timna (near Lydda) figures in the late 1st or early 2nd century, was a Roman military patrol engaged in search and intelligence, and prone, apparently, to predatory behaviour.[98]

Among the types who belonged to the matziqim listed in the midrashim therefore, there are two: the first comprises the Roman veterans and the military, who figure prominently. A hegemon could be any commander; more specifically the prefect of a cohort or a procuratorial governor. The use of the term "cleruch", a survival of the hellenistic period, obviously refers to military settlers, and may merely demonstrate the familiarity of the type in Judaea and the deeprootedness of Greek terms. Most interesting, however, is the reference to "the cleruchs... and the beneficarii" and "the centurions who collect money from both of them." In another passage, Megillat Ta'anit (6), the word translated "collect money" above refers to the act of the military in paying into the treasury money they have seized.[99]

The second group of matziqim comprised Roman aristocrats (or their agents), who have received grants of land in Judaea, presumably from the Emperor, after the Jewish war. We have a direct confirmation in Jewish sources of the presence of a member of this group; this is the Roman matronit who held land near Lydda, and evidently inclining to Judaism, paid R. Hyrcanos son of R. Elie'zer 300 kors of grain in tithes annually.[100] There is good authority that in the provinces, e.g. in Egypt, members of the Roman upper class, more especially relatives and supporters of the imperial family, received extensive estates derived from imperial property.[*][101] Vespasian, as the founder of a new imperial dynasty, would certainly have needed to reward his allies and ensure continued support in a similar fashion. It seems altogether likely, then, that Roman supporters of the Flavians received estates in Judaea granted to them by the Emperor, while the military men who acquired lands there at this time had either received them as official allotments from the government, or had seized them and subsequently gained official confirmation of title.

The association of the matziqim with the state, i.e. their official status, is indicated by several other talmudic sources. For instance we find in M. Baba Qama, X, 5: 'If a man rob his fellow of a field, and matziqim take it, if this is an evil caused by state action, the former shall say to him (the rightful owner), "There is your field", but if it is the robber's doing, he must place another field at his disposal.' The matziqim, therefore, have govern-

---

[*] For the location of place-names mentioned throughout the text, see Map 1, p.99.

ment backing, and nothing can be done against them. On the other hand there seems no doubt that some of these oppressive new proprietors were Jews. Such emerges from Jer. Demai, VI, 25b where we read: "He who rents his ancestral plot from a gentile matziq, tithes (his produce) and pays him."

Tos. Baba Qama, X, 20 states: 'If a man robs (his fellow) of a field, and an anas takes it, he (the robber) shall say to him: "There is your field" ...' indicating that the status of the anas is much the same as that of the matziq. Cases are further cited in which the anas abandons agricultural property before he has harvested its produce, or alternatively remains so long in possession that he is believed to be the real owner.[102]

Alon came to the conclusion that the matziqim were conductores of Roman state land subletting to Jewish coloni. There are indeed not a few references in this period to Jews leasing lands, even those previously of their own families, from gentiles.[103] Confiscation of land by the Lex Cornelia de sicariis et venificis and the conditions under which it could be repurchased are in fact discussed in considerable detail in contemporary halakhah.[104]

It is therefore evident that much wild and unregulated seizure of Jewish lands was taking place after the war of 70, side by side with considerable state confiscation and the distribution of tracts to soldiers and aristocratic supporters of the new imperial house. In many cases the Jewish peasants were forced to rent their former plots as tenants or to become tenants of other men's lands. Payment of crops to centurions and into state granaries also indicates that not a few became coloni on imperial estates and probably on the prata of the Tenth Legion about Jerusalem.[105] Alon's belief,[106] however, that the matziqim were conductores of imperial domain, has less to recommend it. The Roman aristocrats who received estates in grant from the emperor, and the troops who had acquired allotments by assignment or obtained confirmation of their title to tracts they had seized, would have held their property optimo iure, as indeed is evident from the testimony of the midrashim and other rabbinical tractates, that their property could be reacquired by their original owners or by others.[107]

In view of the association of the beginnings and the consequences of the Second Revolt with the so-called Har ha-Melekh or "King's Mountain Country", according to three rabbinical traditions, it would be as well at this point to discuss the character of this tract, which has been the subject of prolonged discussion among Jewish scholars. Midrash Siphre on Deuteronomy (6), which we have already utilized, places it between the south end of the Dead Sea and the Shephelah (foothills) to east of Lydda. M. Shevi'it[109] divides Judaea into three parts, the mountain, the western foothills and the (maritime) plain, linking Har ha-Melekh with the foothills by Lydda. Jer. Shevi'it[110] on the other hand, connects the region with the foothills of Darom, between Lydda and Beth Govrin, but also with the plains of 'Ein Geddi and Jericho.

Other sources[111] mention the name as that of one individual place. Mishrash Gadol to Deut. 28:52 calls it "a large town" (Heb. kerakh - a fortified place) and links it with Bethar. Tos. Demai[112] makes it clear that the area included Yishuv and Sokko (Shweikeh) on the north, in the west of the Mountains of Ephraim, and Antipatris and Patros to the south, the latter being a little north of Lydda. B. Gittin[113] extends the area southward into the Darom. It is evident, therefore, that Har ha-Melekh is a term which may originally have applied to one locality only, but in course of time was extended to a very large area, chiefly the western hillslope of Judaea from Ephraim to Beth Govrin approximately, with an eastern spur stretching to west of the Dead Sea. All the traditions speak of it as thickly populated down to the 2nd century, but it was later inaccessible, at least in part, to Jews.

Ben Tziyyon Luria, in his study of Har ha-Melekh,[114] notes that the name first appears in a list of districts whence produce was obtained for the Temple service; the localities are divided into two distinct groups, one stated explicitly to be chronologically later, and there can be little doubt that it relates to the areas acquired by the Hasmonean expansion. This list includes Har ha-Melekh. As an area, Luria locates it in much the same regions as Buechler, i.e. along the western edge of the Judaean hill-country extending as far north as Wadi 'Ara (Nahal 'Iron); he notes that the locality known as Beth Yannai was also in the region.[115] He concludes that Har ha-Melekh was a collective name applied to the Hasmonean royal estates, more especially to those acquired by Yannai (Alexander Jannaeus). B. Gittin,[116] indeed, attributes to Yannai the mythical figure of 600,000 villages in Har ha-Melekh. Buechler, for his part,[117] thought this attribution as mythical as the number, and that the vast estates implied should be ascribed to Agrippa I, as the Jewish king $\kappa\alpha\tau'\dot{\epsilon}\xi o\chi\dot{\eta}\nu$; but Luria's deduction from the list of Temple produce seems to me to make the earlier attribution valid.[118] The area's connection with the Hasmonaean house would be strengthened if we could accept Luria's view that R. Ele'azar ben Harsum, who is reported to have possessed a thousand villages in the Har ha-Melekh,[119] was the High Priest of A.D. 48-58 and of the Hasmonaean family,[120] but Buechler was less sanguine on the correctness of Ele'azar's identification with the said high priest, and the date seems too early.

The fate under Roman rule of this very large area of crown land is a complicated and difficult matter. Part was doubtless restored to the possession of the Greek coastal cities rehabilitated by Pompey. Herod presumably inherited much of the rest, and a tract of it would have been devoted by him to the furnishing of land for his new city of Antipatris; suggestive in this connection is the name Hirbet Bernike, recorded by Alt between Ras el-'Ayyin (Antipatris) and Jaljulia.[121] What remained must have gone to the Roman state on the deposition of Archelaus (A.D. 6), but here again generalization is impossible; Antipas, for instance, held domain in the toparchy of Narbatta.[122] From this bloc of royal domains Herod may well have allotted tracts for the territory of his new city of Caesarea Maritima. Ele'azar ben Harsum inherited his own estates from his father,[123] and appears to have held them down to Hadrian's time. Whether Agrippa I or II retained parts of the property in Har ha-Melekh is problematic (but cf. Hirbet Bernike, above), but as Agrippa I ruled the whole of Judaea, it is reasonable to suppose that he reacquired most of them. It may however be assumed with some confidence that the lands attached to the centres which had been actively implicated in the great rebellion were seized for the praedium Caesaris (Antipatris, Jaffa; Apheqa; Lydda; Narbattene). The probability that after 70, various moderates among the Jewish scholars received land from Vespasian at Lydda, where the Hasmonaeans had acquired rights,[124] indeed suggests that the domains had persisted as an administrative entity; it is very tempting to interpret the χώρα which Vespasian retained for himself in Judaea after 70[125] as simply the Har ha-Melekh, the equivalent of the χώρα βασιλική. Two things, at any rate, can be taken as evident. A number of estates in the area were made over or left to owners original or new - including Jews; and some of them were very extensive, and worked by tenants.[126] The other recipients would have belonged to the category of military settlers described by the midrashim.

In all, Jewish sources evidence a widespread expropriation of the Jewish peasantry and the dire exploitation of those who were allowed to remain on their farms, whether as coloni of praedium Caesaris or as tenants of new proprietors.

Some of the documents recovered among the finds associated with Ben Kosba in the caves of Murabba'at and Naḥal Ḥever have a direct bearing on the above survey. They include several lease-contracts drafted between Jewish officials of Ben Kosba's government and other Jews, for the leasing of lands held by the Jewish revolutionary administration. These are:

1. From Murabba'at, a contract of the year A.D. 133,[127] whereby the official Hillel ben Garis leases land to six Jews resident, apparently, in the town of Naḥash. The land is leased for five years for rent in kind after the discharge of tithe and payment of a further tenth to the treasury.

2. From the Cave of the Letters (Naḥal Ḥever), a contract of A.D. 139,[128] leasing land to a Jewish cultivator; the rent is to be paid in cash.

3. From the same provenance: a receipt[129] issued by one of Ben Kosba's officials for rent paid by a Jew on land leased from the government.

4. A contract for the year A.D. 133,[130] dividing among four Jews land leased by them at 'Ein Geddi from Ben Kosba's administration.

5. A contract of A.D. 135[131] signed between two of the four lessees assignant to (4), whereby the first of them leases out a plot leased to himself. One of the witnesses to the document is an official of Ben Kosba's government.

6. A contract between two of the assignants to contract 5,[132] whereby they lease to a third party part of the land rented by document 4.

It is evident from the above that Ben Kosba as secular head of the revolutionary administration of Judaea was vested with the control of various lands, some of which he rented out.[133] It can be deduced from the documents found in both caves, however, that not all the soil of Judaea under the new régime was state-property, since several records from Murabba'at are deeds of sale of lands transferred without government mediation.[134] The lands under Ben Kosba's control, therefore, constituted a distinct category.

It is impossible to know from these few surviving leases what was their extent, but two hints might be interpreted to mean that they were considerable:

1. One of the plots rented was at Naḥash, near Eleutheropolis (Beth Govrin) in the south-west of Judaea;[135]

2. The various leases were granted in the course of a period of three years (133-135).[136]

It would be reasonable to suppose, then, that the estates concerned fell into three categories: a) abandoned tracts whose previous Jewish owners had been killed or died subsequently to 70 and left no heirs; b) lands of non-Jews; and c) Roman state-lands not held by Jewish sub-lessees subsequent to the same year. In respect of this last category, it is not without significance that the lease stipulated in one of these contracts is for five years (a Roman lustrum), the period usual in similar leases on Roman state-lands.[137]

It may therefore be tentatively suggested on the basis of the talmudic evidence and of the documents cited above, that the problems of land and tenure were among the chief factors that preoccupied the Jews who took part in the second revolt, and were among its chief causes.

THE RURAL TRADITION

A group of talmudic traditions connected with the outbreak and results of the war are indeed such as to indicate that the Second Jewish Revolt took its origin first and foremost among the rural elements of the population.

1. The already cited passage on the thousand villages of R. Ele'azar ben Ḥarsum in Har ha-Melekh (Jer. Ta'anit, IV, 8 69a): There were ten-thousand villages in Har ha-Melekh, and R. Ele'azar ben Ḥarsum had a thousand of them, and also a thousand ships, and all of them were destroyed.

2. A story that purports to explain why Har ha-Melekh came to be destroyed (B. Gitt. 55b). It was traditional to send a cock and a hen before a bridal pair as a symbol of fertility. A Roman military unit passing by laid hands on the birds, so provoking the retaliation of the peasants, under the leadership of one Bar Daroma, whose exploits against Hadrian as described here, are such as to equate him in function if not in person with Ben Kosba himself.

3. A passage which explains the destruction of Bethar as resulting from a clash between the emperor's daughter and its villagers. It was the local custom to plant a cedar on the birth of a boy, and a pine tree on the birth of a girl; when they were wedded, both trees were used to make the bridal canopy. The emperor's daughter was passing by, the axle of her carriage broke, and her attendants took a cedar tree to mend it. They were beaten up by the villagers, whereupon the news was brought to the emperor that the Jews had risen. (B. Gittin, 57a).

4. A passage that explains the destruction of Bethar in a different way. This was because the inhabitants lit candles (i.e. rejoiced) when Jerusalem was destroyed. The reason lay in the fact that the councillors of Jerusalem had made a practice of pestering pilgrims from the village, when they came to town, to become councillors or archons; alternatively to sell their lands. Refused on both counts, they would forge sales contracts whereby the pilgrims found themselves deprived of their lands. (Mid. Lam. R., II, 5 (19)).

5. The tradition of two brothers of Kefar Ḥarubba who slew every Roman who passed their village. On the approach of the Romans they proclaimed their intention to take the crown from Hadrian and set it on the head of Simon. There follows a tradition concerning their death at the hands of the Romans strongly resembling a parallel passage relating to Simon ben Kosba. (Mid. Lam. R, II, 5 (19)).

6. Jer. Berakhot II, 5a, tells the story, transmitted to R. Yudan by R. Eibo, that a Jew was ploughing when his ox lowed, and a passing Arab cried: "Jew, put away your ox and your ploughshare, for the Temple is destroyed." The ox lowed again, whereupon the Arab cried: "Jew, tie up your ox and your ploughshare, for the King Messiah is born." He said to him: "What is his name?" (The Arab replied) "Menahem". He said to him: "And what is the name of his father?". He replied: "Hezeqiah." He said to him: "Whence comes he?" He said to him: "From the royal city of Bethlehem in Judaea." A parallel version in Mid. Lam. R., I, 57 (17), has "the fortress of 'Arvah of Bethlehem in Judaea" - mentioned as Qiriat 'Arviyah in the Murabba' at and Naḥal Ḥever documents.[138]

7. Mid. Gadol to Deut. 28:52 mentions the Har ha-Melekh and Bethar in association. Jer. Ma'aser Sheni, I, 2 52b, refers to a Qastra (fort) at Har ha-Melekh. (Cf. also Tos. Ma'as. Sh., I, 5-6). Both passages relate to conditions after Hadrian's time.

It may be commented on the above passages, that they have an essentially rural background. Various other rabbinical passages on Har ha-Melekh not cited here, indeed, refer to the agricultural produce of the area.[139] 2, 3, 4 and 6 are most pronouncedly stories about peasants. Secondly, 2, 3 and 5 represent direct clashes between the peasants and the Roman power, in two cases with the military, in one case with the emperor's daughter. 4, the most interesting of these traditions, bears a different character from the rest; it belongs less to the folklore genre, and is more circumstantial. But it also presents difficulties, for it appears to contain several strata. It deals, ostensibly, with events before the destruction of Jerusalem in 70, yet purports to explain why Bethar was destroyed in 135. The alleged defrauding of peasants of their lands by Jerusalem aristocrats could only have taken place before 70; on the other hand the rôle of the councillors who pester pilgrims from Bethar to become councillors and archons is characteristic rather of conditions in the 3rd and 4th centuries.[140] The basic elements of value in this tradition, I think, are the antagonism between the urban and rural populations which had earlier found expression in the rebellion of 66-73, and the memory, overlaid by later experiences, that the second revolt had been associated with the rural elements.[141] (6), recording the inception of a messianic movement near Bethlehem, in the heart of the area shown by coin-finds to have been the initial focus of the rebellion of 132, hardly requires further comment. The association with Hezeqiah and Menahem constitutes the awareness of a link between the Sicarian movement founded by Judah of Galilee and the rising of Ben Kosba. The location of the messianic event at Qiriat 'Arviyah by the <u>Midrash Lamentations</u> tradition, suggests that this place, whether Ḥirbet 'Ariv or el-'Ariv near Bethlehem, may have been the Kefar Ḥarruba where(5) places the proclamation of Ben Kosba as "king."

The important conclusion to be drawn from the above sources is, that practically all the traditions connected with the origin and progress of the second revolt can be located in the rural areas, including Har ha-Melekh. Passage 5, associates with Kefar Ḥarruba the crystallization of the rising about the leadership of Ben Kosba. The character of the rising as a preponderantly peasant movement is confirmed by the absence of the record of any major town in connection with the events of the war, with the exception of Jerusalem, whose precise rôle in them is still controversial (See p. 27). It is further confirmed by the information of Dio of the capture of fifty fortresses and 985 villages by the Roman forces engaged in suppressing the rising.[141a] The question of the reliability of Dio's figures will be discussed below.

In general, the view that the revolt took its initial impetus from peasant discontent engendered by expropriation and oppressive tenurial conditions intensified by a strong messianic mood, would answer very well to the term applied by at least one source to the rising, viz. $\varkappa \text{ίνησις}$,[142] which means, <u>inter alia</u>, a political movement,[143] or even a revolution.[144]

PRIOR UNREST

It is probable that the Jewish insurrection of 132 did not break out suddenly, but grew out of a prolonged period of unrest which increasingly assumed the character of guerrilla warfare. The evidence consists of talmudic references to incidents involving <u>listim</u>, i.e. brigands, records relating to movements of Roman military units, and of archaeological data.

It seems that Judaea continued to be disturbed periodically during the entire period from 73 to 132. It has been pointed out that the Cohors I Augusta Lusitanorum, was in Judaea in 86, when personnel from this and other units were granted citizenship on the conclusion of twenty years' service, but were not released.[145] In 103 or 107 Claudius Atticus Herodes put to death Simon son of Cleopas head of the Jerusalem Christian community and reputed descendant of David, thus suspected of messianic aspirations.[147] Syme has noted the anomalous third praetorian governorship served by Atticus' successor Q. Pomponius Falco in Judaea in 107/8,[148] and its possible connection with local disorders in the country. It is worthy of note that Camp 'F2' at the foot of Masada appears to have been evacuated about 111, when a hoard of coins was deposited there.[149] The gun platforms of this fort (see below, p. 29) are surely the best evidence that this part of Judaea remained disturbed for some time after 73, when Masada fell.[149a]

How far there were serious disorders in Judaea during the Diaspora insurrection of 115-117 cannot be discussed at length here. But it is relevant to mention two pieces of archaeological evidence which bear on the question. Dr. Ya'aqov Kaplan, excavating at Jaffa in 1962, reports[150] that the 2nd-century stratum included a building which yielded evidence of destruction; it contained two stamps of a Jewish agoranomos of the year 107, as well as pottery and coins dating the damage to Trajan's reign, and connecting it, in the excavator's view, with the Diaspora rising of 115-117. The evidence of the Falco dedication referred to above, however, might connect this find rather with the supposed disorders of 107. Further evidence comes from Gerasa over the Jordan. Here the architectural fragments of a synagogue incorporated in the triumphal arch erected in honour of Hadrian in 130, were attributed by Dettweiler to destruction occasioned by the great rebellion of 66-73.[151] It is however virtually certain that the Gerasa burnt by L. Annius in 68[152] was not Gerasa of the Decapolis, since this city both protected its own Jewish residents[153] and was attacked by the Jewish insurgents. In consequence some other occasion must be sought for the destruction of the Gerasa synagogue, and the only possible occasion is the revolt of Trajan's time.[154]

Finally, the newly established province of Arabia was apparently in an insecure state in the late 'twenties of the 2nd century. The latest inscription at 'Avdat at this time has been dated to 128,[154a] after which occupation of the town ends for the time being. Abandonment has been found to have occurred in the first century or contemporarily at other central Negev sites along the route from 'Avdat to Moyet Awad. At Mampsis (Kurnub), evidence appears to last to 130.[155] Professor A. Negev attributed the evacuation of 'Avdat to the penetration of Safaitic and Thamudic tribes whose inscriptions are now found in the vicinity of the town of 'Avdat.[156] Professor Gihon, on the other hand, has explained the evacuation of the central Negev as a characteristic Hadrianic act of retrenchment occasioned by the Ben Kosba revolt.[157] Neither hypothesis need contradict the other; the pressure of the nomadic tribes might have drawn in sufficient Roman forces to have enabled Jewish unrest in Judaea to reach the stage of open revolt in 132; equally, the diversion of Roman units to deal with Ben Kosba in the north might have afforded an opportunity to the nomads of breaking into the central Negev and of despoiling its northern settlements. Unfortunately the interpretation of the archaeological evidence on which the hypothesis depends, i.e. the dating of the destruction layer at 'Avdat, is so controversial that at present no firm conclusion is possible.[158] Moreover, evidence from Africa may be connected with the Negev trouble, although certainty is at present impossible. This is a sentence from the famous speech of Hadrian delivered to legion III Augusta in 126.[159] He there refers to the despatch by that legion of reinforcements to another legion numbered III - which could be the III Cyrenaica, probably by then in Arabia, or the III Gallica of Syria. This took place a year before Hadrian's speech was delivered (ante annum), i.e. in 125. It should further be mentioned that a detachment of III Cyrenaica has left an inscription in the cemetery of Mampsis,[160] and another, unfortunately not datable, near Eilat.[161]

Two papyri have also been regarded by scholars as evidence of military activity in Judaea in the years immediately preceding the revolt. The first is Pap. Greci e Latini, PSI, IX, no. 1206, a petition of soldiers discharged in 150 from legion X Fretensis, to which they had been transferred from the Classis Misenensis. They had enlisted in the fleet in 125. After having served in the legion over 20 years, they request to be released as legionaries and not as marines. It follows that their transfer had taken place in 129/130, which implies that the X legion at Jerusalem stood in need of reinforcements in that year.

The second document (P. Ryland, II, 189),[162] records the receipt of five felt caps from the villagers of Skenopoionesos, for troops serving in Judaea. The date is 128. Alon[163] sees in this requisitioning of clothing an indication of a state of emergency in Judaea, during which normal supplies could not be obtained. I do not find this interpretation very convincing.[164]

So much for the military evidence on the Roman side for a state of unrest between the great rebellion and the rising in Hadrian's time. One further testimony will be cited later on. In the meantime the evidence of Jewish sources relating to the presence of brigandage in Judaea may be referred to. First, Bab. AZ. 25b relates that when the pupils of R. 'Aqiva were journeying to 'Akko, they encountered brigands (listim), who, hearing who they were, cried: "All prosperity to R. 'Aqiva and his pupils, whom no evil man ever injured!" Alon justifiably comments,[165] that brigands who respected the rabbi and his pupils were not simple robbers. A similar interpretation may be put on the case cited by the same historian, of the son of R. Ḥanina ben Teradion (A.D. c. 120-140) who joined brigands, betrayed them and was put to death by them.[166] As R. Ḥanina was a scholar with a comfortable livelihood, it is unlikely that his son took to brigandage for gain, and a political cause is to be suspected. This may also be the meaning of the story of the Galileans who had slain a man and appealed to R. Tarfon (A.D. 120-140) to hide them:[167] likewise of the account of a Jewish brigand caught in Caesarea of Cappadocia, who confessed before his execution that he had killed Simon ben Kahana,[168] a pupil of R. Eli'ezer ben Hyrcanus, a contemporary of R. 'Aqiva, at the entrance to Lydda.[169] The causes of these phenomena were apparently both economic and political, and various evidence can be quoted from rabbinical sources of a difficult economic situation and dire poverty in Judaea in Hadrian's reign.[170]

Of considerable importance for a correct appreciation of the circumstances in which the Jewish rebellion broke out is the evidence to be derived from a milestone discovered near Megiddo in 1960.[171] This was dated to 130 (Hadrian's fourteenth tribunician power and his third consulship), and shows that the construction of the road from Sepphoris to Caparcotna, the station of legion VI Ferrata, was completed in that year, and that the legion had probably arrived at its new base by then, and not after the rebellion, as has been assumed by scholars hitherto. Such a move, moreover, would have implied the parallel and proportionate reinforcement of auxiliary units in Judaea. (See below, p. 33). Since the above milestone was published, however, another has been found on the Caparcotna-Sepphoris road, dating to A.D. 69 and set up by M. Ulpius Trajan, then legate of legion X Fretensis.[171a] This considerably weakens the value of the milestone of A.D. 130 as an argument for the arrival of VI Ferrata at Caparcotna before that year, but does not completely nullify it; the repair of 130 remains a fact, and Keppie's arguments for the presence of VI Ferrata in Judaea before Hadrian's Jewish war (see note 173) carry considerable weight. See now moreover, Bowersock in JRS LXV, 1975, pp. 183-185, showing that the legion was in Arabia in Hadrian's reign. It should now be added that at least one milestone on the road Scythopolis-Caparcotna is now thought to have been first set up under Hadrian (e.g. Israel Milestone Committee, no. 201 - Mr. Isaak's report no. 13 to the Commission). Isaak further believes that the entire road from Caesarea to Scythopolis was repaired in 130; Hadrian's work is also attested along the Legio-Neapolis route. Izaak writes to me: "My definite impression is that the year A.D. 130 represents the first major road-building project in the province of Judaea."

This new information enables us to evaluate more accurately Dio's description of the beginning of the war. His brief account, the only one we have that conveys any details of the military situation, can be claimed as unreliable because it comes to us in Xiphilinus' abbreviation, but some of its details have proved verifiable, and the general lines make an impression of authenticity. The account opens as follows:

Παρόντος μὲν ἔν τε τῇ Αἰγύπτῳ καὶ αὖθις ἐν τῇ Συρίᾳ τοῦ Ἀδριανοῦ ἡσύχαζον,πλὴν καθ' ὅσον τὰ ὅπλα τὰ ἐπιταχθέντα σφίσιν ἧττον ἐπιτήδεια ἐξεπίτηδες κατεσκεύασαν,ὡς ἀποδοκιμασθεῖσιν αὐτοῖς ὑπ' ἐκείνων χρῆσασθαι,ἐπεὶ δὲ πόρρω ἐγένετο,φανερῶς ἀπέστησαν, καὶ παρατάξει μὲν φανερᾷ οὐκ ἐτόλμων διακινδυνεῦσαι πρὸς τοὺς Ῥωμαίους,τὰ δὲ τῆς χώρας ἐπίκαιρα κατελάμβανον καὶ ὑπονόμοις καὶ τείχεσιν ἐκρατύνοντο ὅπως ἀναφυγάς τε ὁπόταν βιασθῶσιν ἔχωσι καὶ παρ' ἀλλήλους ὑπὸ γῆν διαφοιτῶντες λανθάνωσι,διατιτράντες ἄνω τὰς ὑπογείους ὁδοὺς κτλ..........καὶ τὸ μὲν πρῶτον ἐν οὐδενὶ αὐτοὺς λόγῳ οἱ Ῥωμαῖοι ἐποιοῦντο·ἐπεὶ δ' ἥ τε Ἰουδαία πᾶσα ἐκεκίνητο τότε δὴ τότε τοὺς κρατίστους τῶν στρατηγῶν ὁ Ἀδριανὸς ἔπεμψεν,κτλ 172

This would convey that systematic preparations of an underground character began after Hadrian's departure, and that the actual rebellion broke out somewhat later, yet that even then the Jews did not venture an open attack upon the Romans. The new evidence from Megiddo, makes it possible,however, that latest by 130, when Hadrian was still in Judaea,a new legion had been moved into the province; as no great time can have elapsed between the legion's arrival and the relaying of the Megiddo road, this could have been the result of the Imperator's on-the-spot estimate of the situation, and hardly earlier.173 Dio, in Xiphilinus' version, continues: "At first the Romans paid no attention whatever to all this [sc. the Jewish preparations]. But when entire Judaea was in a state of revolt Hadrian sent his best commanders, the foremost being Julius Severus" etc. Two deductions then may be drawn from Dio's account: 1) As the administration was perfectly aware that trouble was brewing, the claim that the Romans paid no attention to the rising at the beginning is inaccurate, and the account is apologetic. 2) The fact nevertheless remains that the Roman forces, reinforced and ready as they were, could not prevent the rising attaining wide proportions. Taken literally, this was a failure of the intelligence branch; whatever the case, it is clear that there was certainly a failure of reconnaissance work. The actual foci of the rebellion were not located, or if they were located, they were not penetrated and could not be watched. This failure may have led to a false appreciation of the scale of the potential rising.

We shall see below (pp. 43 sq.) that specialist scouting units were a development which took place in the Roman army after the second Jewish revolt. Details of reconnaissance arrangements before that are not known. There does exist, however, some information concerning the state and military intelligence services, particularly in Judaea. On the one hand rabbinical sources evidence the presence in the country of Roman intelligence agents who were active in investigating opinions and practices both before and after the second revolt; one, a quaestor, detects the disciples of R. Meir at secret prayer;[174] another quaestor finds a Jew of Sepphoris examining a mezuzal and extracts from him a bribe or fine of a thousand denarii.[175] An inscription of the legion III Augusta at Lambaesis,[176] indeed, associates a quaestor with the beneficarii consularis, the speculatores, questionarii (of whom see below) and other headquarter staff of the legion. A passage in Mid. Lam. R. II (Buber, p. 98) describes the speculator and the quaestor as acting together, but it is the speculator who hands the victim over to execution. The quaestor who is described in another place as interested in Jewish ritual,[177] therefore, may not have been as friendly as he affected to be.[178] The two stratiotai who paid a study-visit to the rabbinical school of Yavneh in Gamliel's time,[179] were also certainly acting for the authorities, as their remarks indicate. It was Hadrian or Trajan who instituted the frumentarii as intelligence agents both at Rome and in the legions.[180] They and the speculatores also acted as despatch-riders and as special police,[181] investigating and arresting, among others, the Christians.[182] Similar functions may have been discharged by the veredarii,[183] also instituted by Trajan or Hadrian. The II Traiana, III Cyrenaica and X Fretensis, all of which served in Judaea during the war of 132-135, all possessed frumentarii,[183a] while the term speculator found its way into contemporary Hebrew,[184] and speculatores are recorded by the scholars as carrying out summary executions in the course of duty.[185] They were, in fact, a semi-secret police whose summary actions appear to have stood outside the due process of law.

In addition we hear of military patrols (boleshot) visiting villages; the Hebrew term used for them is derived from a root (בלש) meaning "to spy" or "to keep a watch upon"; their duties were nominally fiscal,[186] and they may have included discharged soldiers settled on the land.[186a] The boleshot referred to in Tosephta Betzah was encountered by R. Simon of Timnah who flourished between 80 and 120.[187]

The legion III Cyrenaica, it might be added, possessed a sinister quaestionarius, who left an inscription[188] at Sur in northern Hauran in the time of M. Aurelius or later. Sur (Heb. Ḥalmish) is noted in Jewish sources[189] as a Roman fort which habitually harassed the Jewish town of Neveh. We may note from the Lambaesis inscription cited above,[176] the association of the quaestionarii of III Augusta with the legion's speculatores.

If VI Ferrata was at Caparcotna by 130, the question arises, in which year did the rebellion assume the acknowledged proportions of a war? Milik has interpreted a lease contract from Murabba'at[190] to indicate that the rebellion broke out in 131, as this was the first year of Ben Kosba's coins bearing the declaration of "the redemption of Israel" (גאולה ישראל). This conclusion was reached from the fact that the said lease, drafted in the second year of the redemption of Israel, was for five years, and valid till "the eve of the sabbatical year". According to Milik's calculation, as 68/9 had been a sabbatical year, 135 was also such, hence the year of the lease was the third year of the previous sabbatical cycle, ie. 132/3, which meant that the first year of the redemption fell in 131. However, Milik's calculation appears to be erroneous:[190a] on my own calculation the proximate sabbatical years to the lease fell in 131 and 139, so that the lease was drafted in 133/4, and the first year of the redemption was 132/3, a date supported by Jewish tradition.[191]

There is nevertheless evidence which could mean that trouble had already begun in 131, namely, the appearance in that year of coins on which Hadrian is portrayed in armour.[192] The Murabba'at evidence, if it has been rightly read, shows that by 132 the rebellion had attained sufficient success to enable the striking of numerous revolutionary coins which declared the aim of the movement, and were overstruck on currency derived from a wide area. (See p. 23.) It would therefore appear legitimate to assume that the rising had begun some months before 132. In this connection may be mentioned the military diploma CIL III, 2, no. xl p. 882, the discharge certificate of a man who had enlisted in the Cohors I Vindelicorum at Caesarea Maritima in 132. The cohort which he joined had probably come from Dacia,[193] and was evidently recruiting reinforcements at Caesarea; it is not therefore beyond possibility that it had already incurred losses in Judaea, although this cannot be proved.

THE GEOGRAPHICAL SCOPE OF THE RISING

The question arises, what was the geographical scope of the rising within the province of Judaea. The most comprehensove treatment of the problem has been that of Adolph Buechler,[194] who after a thorough discussion of the talmudic sources concluded that the war was on the whole confined to Judaea in the limited geographical sense, meaning the region centred on Jerusalem, and not the Roman province, which included also Samaria, Galilee and Idumaea. It is nevertheless true that some talmudic passages suggesting that Galilee was involved cannot be completely excluded from consideration.

Yeivin, on the other hand, was convinced that Galilee was party to the rebellion,[195] but this view rested chiefly on his identification of Kefar Ḥarruba, one of its initial centres, with the village of Kefar Ḥarrub east of Lake Kinneret (the Sea of Galilee), and on his association of the destruction of three Jewish loc localities in Galilee (Siḥin, Migdal and Kabul Gavri) as recorded in rabbinical sources,[196] with the period of Ben Kosba. Kefar Ḥarruba, however, is much more likely to have been the site of the same name near Bethlehem, while the destruction of the three Galilean townlets concerned certainly took place in the great rebellion of 66-73, when fighting in the districts of Migdal and Kabul is described by Josephus.[197]

Alon, dealing with the problem of the war-theatre,[198] acknowledged that Buechler had taken the correct view, at least in so far as Judaea was the main focus of hostilities. He further drew attention to the fact that as the principal Jewish centres of learning moved to Galilee after the war, clearly Galilee had not suffered to the extent that Judaea had. He also noted[199] that Tzippori (Sepphoris) was honoured with the titles $\alpha\upsilon\tau\acute{o}\nu o\mu o\varsigma, \pi\iota\sigma\tau\acute{\eta}, \varphi\acute{\iota}\lambda\eta$ under Antoninus Pius, evidencing the city's loyalty to Rome during the revolt.[200] He observed, with Buechler, that all the names traditionally connected with the war are located in Judaea, with the possible exception of Ḥamat, whose position is a subject of controversy.[201] Nevertheless the reference to the scarcity of olives in Galilee since the time of Hadrian, recorded by R. Jose,[202] himself a native of that region, is attributed by him to Roman action, nor can the presence of inscriptions of the legions XIV Gemina at Gadara[203] and the XI Claudia at Scythopolis (Beth Shean)[204] be easily disassociated from contemporary events, although neither place is actually in Galilee. On the other hand the discovery of second-century pottery and a tile bearing the stamp of VI Ferrata near Safed,[205] indicates little more than that the area was under the legion's care, but cannot be further interpreted till more is known of the character of the site. In a recent publication[206] of the literary sources bearing on the question of the extent of the rising, A. Oppenheimer expressed the view that the main rising took place in Judaea, but that there were some manifestations of revolt in Galilee.[206a] Since the problem of the theatre of hostilities was discussed by the above scholars, archaeological research has been able to cast further light on the limits of the rebellion. The most useful contribution has been made by the numismatists. After a thorough survey of the finds-distribution of Ben Kosba's coins in Eretz Yisrael, the late Dr. L. Kadman was able to state[207] that no single find of such coins could be reliably authenticated in the north of the country.[208] Owing to his premature death, the full results of his survey are not now available, but certain prominent features can be defined relating to the distribution of the coinage of the rebellion.

As is well known, this coinage is composed almost entirely of overstruck Roman issues. Among these, issues of Gaza and Ascalon bulk so large that some scholars have no doubt that these two cities were actually held for a time by the insurgents. A few of the bronze coins originated at Tiberias, and the majority of the tetradrachms at Antioch. A number of overstruck denarii of Caesarea of Cappadocia were also in circulation. Minting of local city issues at Tiberias and several other Greek cities of the country, on the other hand, ceased entirely during the war, apparently because of the interference with communications and trade.[209]

The concentration of Ben Kosba's influence in the centre of the country, as demonstrated by coin-distribution, is probably to be explained not only by the presence of VI Ferrata at Caparcotna (Lejjun) near Megiddo, where it was in a position to check any attempt at coordination between the Jews of Galilee and those of Judaea, but also by the presence of a fortified patrol-line evidenced by rabbinical sources between Sepphoris and Tiberias. Tos. 'Erubin, IV, 11 ascribes to R. Simon a statement that it was possible to go from Tiberias to Tzippori (Sepphoris) using only caves and towers as stopping places. The same statement recurs in Jer. 'Erub., V, 22b where however the word burganin (burgi) is substituted for "towers", and the author of the statement is identified as R. Simon bar Yoḥai, who lived under Hadrian and survived the revolt. The road concerned is thought to have been paved, if not previously laid out, under Hadrian, a milestone of 137 being known from its line.[210] It would therefore seem that this route was a patrolled line in Hadrian's time, and the paving of the Tzippori-Caparcotna road in 130[211] makes it probable that the Tiberias-Tzippori highway also belonged to the period of the rebellion, the more so in view of the difficult winter conditions apt to prevail in Lower Galilee. Its strategical potentiality as a means of checking infiltration between Galilee and the south is clear, and the line invites a close archaeological survey.

The coin-evidence relating to Gaza and Ascalon strongly suggests that

Ben Kosba's forces held the south coast of Judaea in the initial period of the war. This probability is enforced by other items of information. 1) The tradition of R. Ele'azar ben Harsum's large holdings in Har ha-Melekh and his thousand ships on the sea, which met their end at this time. As the settlement of Gidra da-Qesarin recorded in Sheb. VII, 10 was in Har ha-Melekh, and near Caesarea,[212] the area must have approached the seacoast of Judaea in that region. Nor is there any doubt that sea-fighting took place in the course of the war. Two well-known inscriptions recording battle-decorations awarded by Hadrian to Roman commanders for naval operations bello Iudaico[213] have usually been assumed to relate merely to the safe transport of troops to the theatre of war, but there are grounds for a different interpretation. Hadrian was extremely parsimonious in his military awards in the latter part of his reign, as Professor Birley has taught us,[214] hence if fleet commanders were decorated in the Jewish war, we may believe that serious fighting by sea did actually take place.[215] And with this, perhaps, we ought to connect the tradition of R. Ele'azar's thousand ships.

There is no certainty how far north along the coastal plain the control of the insurgents extended at this date, but it is clear from inscriptions that Caesarea was held by the Roman government, and served as the principal base for ultimate counter-operations. The occupation of Tell el-Qasile on the Yarqon just north of Tel Aviv, is interrupted in the earlier Roman period,[216] but it is uncertain whether the interruption was caused by the first or the second revolt. The Tel Aviv University excavations at Antipatris in the years 1972-3 have shown that the city was destroyed in the Jewish war of 66-73 and not reoccupied before the time of Severus. This being the case, the interrupted occupation at Tell el-Qasile is probably to be ascribed to the same cause. The extension of Har ha-Melekh through the Sharon would make it possible that the Jews held the latter territory;[217] on the other hand the small area excavated at the Roman village of Tell Ibrekhtas south of Hadera revealed no evidence of interrupted occupation at this time; it continued at least into the 3rd century, so that it may be tentatively concluded that the Jewish hold ceased south of the Hadera river. The nervousness of the Roman administration as regards the northern coastal plain may nevertheless be reflected in the Roman fort found a few years ago at Sycaminum (Tell es-Sumak);[218] it was occupied from Hadrian's time down to the 3rd century, and commanded the narrow passage along the coast round Carmel to Haifa. It is indeed possible that in the initial stages the Jews, though they had no foothold on the coastal plain of Samaria, controlled the Carmel area above it.[219].

There is very little doubt, however, that the main centre of the Jewish movement was south of Jerusalem, in the Hebron area; so much is clear from the intense concentration of coins of Ben Kosba in that region. Precisely when the latter fixed his headquarters here we do not know, but hoards, the latest Roman coins in which are of the year 131, in this area (already referred to) suggest that it was early in the war, and it seems entirely logical to suppose that the revolt was first prepared in that neighbourhood, since only there did the optimum physical conditions exist to enable secret preparations that were beyond the ability of the Roman forces to observe. In the year 132, on the evidence of a Murabba'at document,[219a] one of the Jewish government's administrative centres was at Herod's fortress and burial place, the Herodium (El-Furedis).

These circumstances, and the discoveries in the caves of the Judaean Wilderness, have led to what may be called a minimalist view of the area of the revolt. This is represented in its sharpest form by G. Förster,[220] who believes that the limits of the movement were marked by Jerusalem and Ramallah on the north, by Bethar on the west, and by the west shore of the Dead Sea on the east. This area contains the majority of the places mentioned in the documents of Murabba'at and Naḥal Hever - 'Ein Geddi, Teqoa', Herodium, Masada, Metzad Ḥassidim, Beth Batza, Gophna etc. and probably some places connected with the revolt in other sources (e.g. Bethel = ? Bethlehem; Kefar Leqitya = ? Ḥirbet el-Qeta). (See p. 55.) Among them are also Kuzeiba, which could have been Ben Kosba's place of origin, and Qiriat 'Arviyah, which Förster identifies with Kefar 'Arub (see above).

Clearly the above estimate of the area affected by the war encounters grave objections, such as the known distribution of Ben Kosba's coinage, the traditions allegedly connecting some villages in the Beth Govrin district of south-western Judaea with the war,[221] the evidence for sea-fighting, and the references to the association of Ele'azar ben Ḥarsum with the rising. We also have to consider the 985 Jewish villages and 50 strongholds alleged by Dio[222] to have been captured during the suppression of the revolt, and the very large Roman force which it was found necessary to employ to bring the war to a conclusion.[223] There may also be some archaeological evidence which could be interpreted to point to the Jewish-held area as extending well over south-western Judaea. (Hebron-Beth Govrin-Gaza). This is the finds-area of clay lamps of late Herodian type, many of which bear the menorah symbol. They date from the post-Destruction period, and last till the rising of 132.[223a] The distribution is in south-west Judaea centring on Beth Govrin, Govrin, which lay on the west perimeter of the Roman road-system encircling Bethar. It would be reasonable to see in the emergence of these lamps, distinctly Jewish and bearing symbols of the Temple cult, a reflection of the revolutionary movement, the more so since this writer has long held the view that certain Jewish lamps found and made in Cyrene, and bearing the menorah symbol, dating as they do between 70 and 115, can be connected with other appearances of the symbol in that province and represent Jewish revolutionary propaganda.[223b] Some lamps of the Judaean group, moreover, bear agricultural tools and plants in place of the menorah motif, thus according well with our contention that the revolt was born first and foremost in the rural districts of the country. All in all, it seems desirable at present to avoid a dogmatic view on the problem of the initial geographical extent of the Jewish movement.

MILITARY CONSIDERATIONS

It is fairly evident from the few salient facts known to us of the course of the war, that the Roman forces faced serious difficulties in suppressing the revolt, and that their efforts to do so only began to bear fruit after the arrival of one of Hadrian's best marshals, Julius Severus, in 133/4 or 134/5.[224]

Salient events of the period prior to Severus' arrival were: 1) The calling in of reinforcements, probably a legion and its auxilia, from Syria. 2) Heavy Roman losses, generally believed to have included the legion XXII Deioteriana; it has recently been suggested that the IX Hispana, which for many years was considered to have been lost in Britain, actually met its end at this time in

Judaea, but this possibility has now been shown to be unacceptable by new epigraphical evidence. 3) The possible capture of Jerusalem by the Jewish forces. If the capture took place, it would have been in the course of phase 2 or 3 that they reached the south-west coast of Judaea, since the insurgents are unlikely to have left the Tenth Legion intact in their rear. 4) The arrival of Severus coincided with, or involved, the concentration of very considerable forces in the country, consisting of a large number of units, legionary and other, from other provinces of the Empire. 5) Possibly at this stage the recapture was effected of the coastal plain by the landing of reinforcements brought by sea, in cooperation with other Roman forces already in the country. Alternatively the maritime plain might have been previously recovered by forces already in Judaea. 6) A slow cautious reduction of the Jewish-held hill country, ending with the investment and capture of Bethar. 7) The reduction of the last strongholds of the rebellion in the Judaean Desert.

Before we attempt a discussion of the tactical implications of the above phases, two controversial questions require discussion. 1) The alleged destruction of XXII Deioteriana, and the possibility that IX Hispana also found its end in Judaea. 2) The alleged capture of Jerusalem by the insurgents.

The evidence suggesting the annihilation of XXII Deioteriana in the revolt falls under two heads: documentary and literary. The legion is last heard of in 119,[225] when it was stationed at Alexandria. It is no longer in the Roman army list found in two copies at Rome, which cannot be later than 162.[226] As Egypt is next door to Judaea, it is reasonable to suppose that the legion was destroyed in the Jewish war. The literary evidence comes from Julius Africanus, who reports that the legion's wine was said to have been poisoned "by the Pharisees".[227] Africanus himself served in the X Fretensis at Aelia Capitolina, where he was born, and probably had heard a regimental tradition which he was ready enough, as a Christian, to credit. The story is more likely to have been apologetic, but it does have the value of establishing that the legion met its end in the Jewish war.

The problem of the IX Hispana is more complex, and has been discussed for decades. The belief that the legion fell a victim to the Britons in about 119[228] has been abandoned in recent years in the face of growing evidence that the legion was at Nijmegen probably by a year variously suggested to be 117, 122 or 126.[229] As there is epigraphical evidence suggesting that the legion was subsequently in an eastern province,[230] Professor Eric Birley[231] believed that it was destroyed either in Judaea or later by the Parthians in 161 in the disaster of Elegeia referred to by Dio.[232] Since no other legion drops out of the Roman army list in this period, Professor Birley, while cautious, appeared to favour the second solution.

A good deal turns on the date of the twin inscriptions found in Rome, that list the legions of the Empire in geographical order in the second half of the 2nd century.[233] The XXII Deioteriana, as stated, and the IX Hispana also, are absent from this record, which must be before 165, when II and III Italica were raised and their names added at the foot of the inscriptions. Indeed, it is unlikely that it was later than 162, since I Minervia, II Adiutrix and V Macedonica here appear at their Hadrianic stations in Lower Germany, Lower Pannonia and Lower Moesia respectively, whereas that year they went eastward to the Parthian War. It is thus chronologically possible that IX Hispana was cut to pieces in 161, but the decision is very much on balance, and Parker, for instance, believed[234] that the lists were of the reign of Antoninus Pius. Fronto's famous statement on the army's heavy losses in Hadrian's time must also be borne in mind, although it seems to me that the words Hadriano imperium obtinente[235] in that passage are just as likely to refer to the losses incurred at Jewish hands in the Diaspora revolt which was still raging on Hadrian's accession. The question has finally been settled in favour of the later contingency, it would seem, by W. Eck,[236] who has shown that a new military diploma[237] which dates the consulship of Q. Numisius Junior in 161, proves him to have been tribunus militum of the IX Hispana in 140/141, thus excluding the possibility of the legion's annihilation in the Jewish war of 132-135.

The problem of whether Jerusalem was reoccupied by the Jews under Ben Kosba is no less complex. Several sources refer to its capture and destruction by Hadrian, among them Appian, whose evidence is that of a contemporary and whose language is unequivocal.[238] The testimony of the Jewish revolutionary coinage, though eloquent, is not quite definite to my own mind: the image of the Temple, its vessels and its festive symbols are all there; but in Years 1 and 2 of the Jewish revolutionary commonwealth the legends are "of or for the freedom of Israel" and "of or for the redemption of Israel", while "for [or of] the freedom of Jerusalem" appears only on issues of Year 3.[239] Kindler has interpreted the last as indicating that Jerusalem, held by Ben Kosba in the first two years of the war, had been recaptured by the Romans by the third.[240]

The archaeological evidence, as it stands, however, is not in favour of a Jewish reoccupation of the capital. In the first two years of excavation outside the west and south walls of the Temple of Jerusalem, conducted since 1967, of the 15,000 coins found, only one was of Ben Kosba.[241] One item of epigraphical evidence, which came to light seventy years ago, could nevertheless be interpreted to furnish grounds for believing that Jerusalem was retaken by the Roman forces towards the end of the war. This is a fragmentary inscription from the city, including the names of three legions, the X Fretensis, the II Traiana,[242] and the XII Fulminata, and therefore clearly of Hadrian's time. It was found with another fragment (A) bearing a dedication to Hadrian, in a tomb to the north of the city reused in the 4th century or later.[242a] There is no reason to see these two fragments as part of one inscription, and fragment B is clearly an epitaph. As the names of the three legions on the latter come after the name of a freedman who presumably set up the epitaph to his late master, they are more probably to be connected with some participation by men of these legions in the act of commemoration than with the career of the deceased soldier. The II Traiana and the XII Fulminata were in Judaea for the war only, and their joint dedication with X Fretensis, were it certain, would evidence a successful action of importance near the city where it was set up.[243]

*   *   *

Judaea (here the entire province including Galilee is meant) consist of much mountain and little plain. The main and easiest lines of movement are from north to south, along the east and west sides of the mountain massif of Samaria and Judaea; a third north-south route is the Judaea-Samaria watershed road which forms the backbone of the country; on this Jerusalem is situated. To north of Samaria, the Vale of Jezreel puts the coastal plain in touch with the Jordan Rift and is at once an indispensable corridor between the two blocks of mountain-country and an approach for penetration of Galilee and Samaria-Judaea. There are few good ports on the coast, so that most invasions must come from the north or the south. These lines of march, however, are exposed to flank-attack from the hills that watch them. The predominantly broken hilly character of the country restricts the field of fullscale battles and more especially of cavalry operations. The penetration of the mountain region is made difficult by the prevalence of defiles and the domination of the routes by higher ground; its control, by the fragmentation of the massif into numerous small independent regions cut off from one another by narrow valleys and defiles. The ascent of the eastern scarp of the massif from the Jordan Valley is particularly risky from a tactical point of view.

The topographical fragmentation of the hill country here referred to faces a ruling power dependant on military force to control the country with the problem of how to do so without the utilization of very large forces and the expenditure of excessive sums on the building and maintenance of numerous military and police posts.

In respect of Judaea an immediate historical and military question arises: what was the size and deployment of the Roman forces in Judaea prior to the rising of 132, firstly down to some year not later than 130, in which the garrison was drastically reinforced, and secondly, after that reinforcement had taken place, but before the despatch of massive expeditionary forces under Julius Severus? It must also be established whether the auxiliary units were brigaded with the legions or whether they were dispersed throughout the country, and if the latter, where?

No survey seems to have been made to ascertain to what extent Judaea possessed permanently occupied Roman forts before the Diocletianic reform,[244] (concerning whose results we have the Notitia Dignitatum Orientis),[245] if we exclude the southern frontier region, and there too our information is still in an incipient stage.[246]

Let us essay a first tentative summary of the slender information at our disposal.

1) A Roman unit was stationed at Tzippori (Sepphoris) in Galilee in the time of Agrippa II, and its castra and hipparchos or hyparchos are mentioned in talmudic halakha.[247] This was shortly before 70. It is unfortunately not ascertainable from the Hebrew text whether the officer of the unit mentioned was a hipparchos or a hyparchos. What may be said is that the term ἔπαρχος is common on inscriptions of the officers of Agrippa II's forces in Bashan and Hauran,[248] and clearly means prefect, usually of an infantry cohort. This might be taken to mean that the term involved at Tzippori did not denote that rank; on the other hand hyparchos is also sometimes used in the Roman period to translate the Latin term prefect.[249] Accordingly it is impossible to decide whether the Roman force stationed at Tzippori was a cavalry or an infantry unit. It can however be stated that the terrain about

Tzippori is not favourable to cavalry, further, that the unit referred to in Tosephta must have been transferred elsewhere before 70, since the town was occupied by Josephus,[250] received a garrison from Cestius Gallus,[251] and another at the end of the war from Vespasian's commander Placidus,[251a] consisting of 500 infantry.[252]

2) A castrum is referred to at Tiberias in the Jerusalem Talmud, by R. Rish Laqish, who lived in the 3rd century.[252a] It stood among demolished buildings. It cannot be shown that this existed earlier, but the inscription of a legionary of VI Ferrata from the town,[253] certainly not pre-Hadrianic, is stated to be before Severus, so that the existence of the fort here during the war is possible, and indeed probable in the view of the evidence cited above that Tiberias stood at the east end of a Hadrianic military road equipped with burgi.

3) G. Schumacher recorded the outline of a fort at el-Jelemmeh south-east of Lejjun, the Roman Caparcotna.[254] This site appears to be that occupied by the present police-station. Its approximate area would appear to have been 1.8 hectares or $4\frac{1}{2}$ acres, which might have held a cohors miliaria or an ala. It is clear from Schumacher's map that this fort was preceded by two earlier camps; parts of two sides of each only are marked, but as both were outside the smaller enclosure referred to above, they were very large and almost certainly legionary marching camps, rather than the permanent fortified base of VI Ferrata, which probably lay to the west some way south of the site of the Roman town of Maximianopolis.[255] 130 would therefore constitute a terminus ante quem for the fort at el-Jelemmeh and it might have been earlier.

4) Sycaminum, today Tell es-Samuk on the coast south of Haifa. A fort was found here by Dr. Y. Algabish during excavations of the ancient town in 1965.[256] It was represented by a stretch of wall 19.5 m long and one metre thick, preserved to a height of $1-1\frac{1}{2}$m. This appeared to be the south wall of the fort. It was joined by several other walls at right-angles. No floor-levels survived and the major part of the structure, which lay on the ridge of the tell, had been destroyed by erosion and by Byzantine building. The main finds associated with the fort were clay lamps, which enabled approximate dating: 1st-century occupation was here superseded by the fort at the beginning of the 2nd century, and demolition had taken place in the middle of the 3rd. "It could be stated with near-certainty that the fort was built between the first Jewish revolt and the rising of Bar Kokhba, and apparently nearer to the latter." A coin of Julia Mammaea represented the height of the occupation. Dr. Algabish believed that the fort was connected with the province's reorganization after the Second Revolt. Its destruction is probably to be associated with the disasters of the third quarter of the 3rd century C.E.

5) Jaffa. According to a stamped tile found in the Roman stratum of Trajan's time (see above), a detachment of X Fretensis must have been at Jaffa contemporarily; whether it continued to be stationed there in Hadrian's time is unknown.

6) Camp F2, at the western foot of Masada, was found by a test excavation conducted by Professor Y. Yadin in 1964-65[257] to have been held from about 73 to 111. F2 occupied the south-west corner of the larger Camp F

built for the siege of 73, and its rampart was equipped with eleven platforms, presumably for artillery.[258] As they belonged to the second period after the siege, and artillery was confined to legionary units,[259] they show that the camp was then held in part by legionaries; the rest of the garrison consisted of cavalry.

7) At Tell Shalem, 10 kilometres south-by-east of Beth Shean, a monumental inscription has been found recording a vexillation of the VI legion Ferrata. It does not predate the 2nd century. Considerable remains of ancient buildings are reported from the immediate vicinity. This site bore the same name in antiquity;[259a] it stands on the Roman road from Beth Shean southward along the Jordan Valley to the Dead Sea; on its east it faces the point where the Yavesh gorge debouches into the Jordan from the mountains of Gilead. The inscription certainly indicates the existence of a permanent fort, and the vexillation would have been in a favourable position to check any move on the part of Jewish forces working northward from the Dead Sea or Lake Kinneret, and to cover the approach to Beth Shean. A bronze statue of Hadrian was found on this site in 1975; it represented the emperor in later life, and clad in a cuirass. G. Förster has suggested that the combat of Romans and barbarians represented on his breastplate may symbolize the struggle with the Jews (Qadmoniot, VIII, 1975, pp. 38-40, Heb.). It seems reasonable to suppose that the statue could only have been erected after the end of the war, and that it adorned the principia of the fort. With it was found the head of a bronze statue of a young girl, whose style was reminiscent of a hellenistic school. Generally these statues would imply that Tell Shalem continued to be garrisoned for several decades, at least, after the revolt had been suppressed.

8) 'Ein Geddi. A document from the Naḥal Ḥever cave referred to a praesidium at 'Ein Geddi and to a Cohors I miliaria Thracum stationed there.[260] The military bathhouse excavated here in 1965 was in use, according to coin-finds, from 70 to the time of Hadrian,[261] and would have belonged to the same cohort.

9) Two towers were found by the American expedition of 1949-51 on the north tell, Tell 2, of hellenistic and Roman Jericho. The later structure was used in the late Roman period. The excavators appear to have been unable to decide whether the earlier tower belonged to the time of Vespasian or of Hadrian,[262] nor is the arrangement of the published pottery such as to make it possible to identify the material associated with the said structure in order to establish whether Hadrianic material was present. Burning attributed to the Second Revolt was found in a Roman house built over the Herodian palace at Tellul Abbu el-Aleiq and excavated in 1975.[262]

10) The centre of the village of 'Azzoun, in western Samaria, 10 kilometres east of Qalqilia, is dominated by a flat-topped hill with a wide command. At its foot has been found the epitaph of a Roman veteran who died in the later 2nd or 3rd century AD.[263] The site is strategically important, occupying as it does a crossroads; topographically it bears a strong resemblance to the position of the Scottish fort of Falkirk. As the hill of 'Azzoun is occupied by a former Jordanian military camp, it can hardly be hoped that traces of the suspected Roman fort survive.[263a]

11) A rooftile with the stamp of legion VI Ferrata was found in a pit at Hurvat Hazon, west of Merom in Galilee.[263c] The pit in question was connected with another, containing a quantity of Roman pottery commencing in the 1st century AD but preponderantly of the 2nd and 3rd century. The excavator, D. Bahat, concluded that most of it looked earlier than the typical 3rd century groups, and that the tile was contemporary with it. "Herodian" lamps, which are generally not later than the Second Revolt, occurred among the material. In the present state of knowledge the existence of a fort here cannot be considered as certain.

12) A small fort measuring 25 by 25 metres and yielding 2nd-century pottery is reported near Nahal Eitan in the Golan (Israel grid, 2264/2634). A burial with a Roman sword of Celtic type (a spatha?) was found at one corner of the fort.[263d]

Not all the above forts are known to have been occupied on the eve of the Second Revolt; one (Masada) certainly was not, nor were they all those that existed. We know of units stationed in various towns and forts just before or during the rebellion of 66-73, and some may have continued to hold these posts. There was a force of cavalry and infantry at Ascalon in 66;[264] there was a permanent garrison at the seat of government, Caesarea.[265] The cavalry veterans settled at Gabba' Hippeon in western Jezreel were a potential force and proved themselves to be such during the Jewish war.[266] Vespasian stationed mixed cavalry and infantry garrisons at Jaffa,[267] Haditta[267a] and at Jericho.[268] We have seen evidence that el-Jelemmeh by Lejjun was garrisoned before Hadrian. It is now known that Roman forts were located on the Nabataean border at Tell Saba (Tell Beersheba) and Tell el-Milik (Moleatha).[269] In addition there were the old Maccabean and Herodian fortresses, concentrated chiefly in eastern Judaea (Herodium, Hyrcania, Alexandreum, Cypros, Threx),[270] of whose occupation we know little or nothing; Masada was garrisoned till 66.[270a]

Those stations whose existence can be postulated on archaeological evidence fall into two groups: city-garrisons and independent forts. Their number is sufficient to show that permanent auxiliary forts existed in Judaea before the Jewish rising under Hadrian. Theoretically, there would have been at least five, since Diploma XIX of AD 86[270b] records two alae and three cohorts stationed in Judaea. It might be permissible tentatively to place alae at el-Jelemmeh and in the Lydda area; the disposition of the infantry units is anyone's guess; one cohort may have been at Tiberias, but the garrison of that town could equally have been a legionary detachment. Even reckoning such legionary detachments,[271] the total force, if this is what Diploma XIV represents, was inadequate,[272] more especially if one considers the Negev border and that from 106/7 Provincia Arabia required a garrison. It would be more reasonable to suppose, that the five units of Diploma XIV were about half the contemporary Judaean garrison, as twelve would be the number needed by one legion (X Fretensis). The diploma may indeed list the northern command, as the Thracians at 'Ein Geddi were not identical with the II Thracum Syriaca recorded by it. Clearly there were reshufflings and transfers in the first decades of the 2nd century: this is the evidence from Masada, while the Cohors I Augusta praetoria Lusitanorum, present in Judaea in AD 86, was in Egypt by 111,[273] when Masada was perhaps evacuated by its garrison.

To the reinforcement of the army of Judaea just before the rising we shall return: in the meantime let us consider the implication of dispersed garrisons. We have emphasized that the Judaean hill country is highly fragmented; between the more negotiable valleys that constitute the local and crosscountry communications are dozens of virtual "islands" of high country, not easily accessible, sometimes partly plateau, often jagged and always rocky; frequently rockstrewn. To what extent they were wooded or bush-covered will be discussed shortly. Many of the steep hillsides were terraced for agriculture and plantations, which made them a little more accessible but also easily blocked and easier to defend, as each terrace was covered by the one above it. They made attack by cavalry almost impossible. The average hill village, moreover, stands, not on a valley-route, but on the hillside, where one part of the houses is commanded by the next. Such country could only be controlled by policing the valley-routes, but actually to penetrate and to dominate the hill-villages required a large and highly specialized force. The risks run by patrols penetrating to them in times of unrest are perhaps illustrated by the already quoted traditions connected with Kefar Ḥarruba, Har ha-Melekh and Bethar.[274]

In the light of this reality it is not difficult to understand how the second revolt could be prepared without the knowledge of the military or at least without their ability to intervene.[275] The military implications of the situation are clear enough: a heavily armed legion in these circumstances would be confined to the main roads, and if its units penetrated the hills, they would sacrifice the principal advantages which endowed the legion with its tactical superiority - massed formation, adequate armour, the pilum volley and the gladius used as opposed masses came to close quarters. Light-armed troops were needed, and in large numbers. If the legion became separated from its auxilia in the mountainous country, moreover, its position might become precarious. The predicament of Cestius Gallus' legions at Beth Horon could easily repeat itself.

It is therefore relevant to enquire how far it was the practice in this period for legions and auxiliary units to be stationed together. That they operated together in the field on various occasions is well-known and need not be emphasized; the question is how far they were held together permanently, since it was the inter-campaign situation that counted when a complete area became involved in a simultaneous rising or in a guerrilla war in which no one combined and numerous body of the enemy could be singled out.

The quartering of a legion and three auxiliary units in one fortress is attested for <u>Novaesium</u> (Neuss), but only down to 70.[276] The fortress had at least 75 barrack blocks.

At <u>Moguntiacum</u> (Mainz) nothing appears to be known of the barrack blocks. But the area of the fortress (33.75 has) is very large, and it held two legions down to 89.[277] According to Baatz, an auxiliary unit may also have been stationed here.[278]

Chester (<u>Deva</u>), with an area of 24.33 has, rebuilt in stone from about 102,[279] does not look, on the basis of what is already known of its barracks, as if there would have been room for auxilia. The epitaph of a trooper of auxiliary cavalry is nevertheless known,[280] but the date is not determinable.[281]

Caerleon (Isca), extending over 20.5 acres and rebuilt in stone in the course of the 2nd century,[282] might have had sufficient room for auxilia, but this has not been suggested.

The following legionary fortresses, excavated wholly or in part, would not appear to have contained space for auxiliary barracks:

Carnuntum (17.6 has); rebuilt in stone from 73;[283] Inchtuthill (21.1 has), occupied c. 83-87;[284] Lauriacum (c. 20 has), rebuilt in stone c. 200;[285] Lambaesis (21.5 has), rebuilt in stone c. 125.[286]

The available evidence for the stationing of auxilia in legionary fortresses after Flavian times, therefore, is not particularly strong. Immediately after the capture of Jerusalem, indeed, Titus left in the city as garrison X Fretensis and several alae and infantry cohorts (τῶν ταγμάτων τὸ δέκατον καὶ τινας ἴλας ἱππέων καὶ λόχους πεζῶν -Jos., BJ. VII, 5). But with a weak provincial garrison it seems unlikely that there were auxiliary units to spare to station in Jerusalem between 70 and 132 unless after exceptional reinforcement from elsewhere, as occurred in 116, when Lusius Quietus' Moorish cavalry numeri were brought to the province, some to Jerusalem.[287]

The transfer of the VI Ferrata to Lejjun in or before 130 would have meant the concomitant increase of the province's auxiliary forces. Some twelve units, including both cavalry and infantry, are to be expected. Wales, a predominantly mountainous country roughly equal in size to Judaea west of Jordan (c. 10,000 square miles) was supervised by two legions. In 103 the Caerleon legionary command in south Wales had 15 auxiliary units - four alae and eleven cohorts, of which two were miliariae, i.e. about 8,500 men. The Chester command in the north, in 98 and 105 included 16 units, comprising four alae and 12 cohorts, some in the western Pennines; one was a cohors miliaria equitata; the total about 8,350 men; of these at least 5,000 were in Wales.[288] In AD 139, after the war, according to Diploma CIX,[289] there were in Judaea 15 units, comprising two alae and 13 cohorts, two miliariae. It is highly improbable that this represented the whole garrison, which now included two legions, but it may well have been the equivalent of the reinforcement of the years close to 130. This would mean that the total auxilia of Judaea at the outbreak of the Jewish war under Hadrian would have constituted approximately 28 units, implying the same number of castella. It is worth recalling that the British Mandatory government between 1936 and 1938 erected some 50 fortified police stations at key-points in Palestine as a result of the Arab revolt of those years; these, however, accommodated the police, who were supplementary to the military forces.

It is fairly evident that the available light-armed units of the garrison of Judaea could do little more than hold the communications through the hill country, but hardly control the intervening village-areas. This contingency would have done much to neutralize the legions as an effective force in the mountain area.

From Dio's brief account of Severus' counterattack against the Jewish forces (as transmitted to us by Xiphilinus), several facts emerge. 1) The Jewish defence was conducted from villages and strongholds, whose numbers are given as 985 and 50 respectively. 2) The number of insurgents was extremely large. 3) Severus' tactic was not to force a frontal battle, but to wear the enemy down by piecemeal isolation and starvation leading to annihilation. One passage, here underlined in the text (LXIX, 13, 3) is singularly difficult to translate, and is suspected of being corrupt, and this is probably a key passage to an understanding of the tactics of Severus' campaign.

ἀντικρυς μὲν οὐδαμόθεν ἐτόλμησε (Severus) τοῖς ἐναντίοις συμβαλεῖν, τό τε πλῆθος καὶ τὴν ἀπόγνωσιν αὐτῶν ὁρῶν· <u>ἀπολαμβάνων δ' ὡς ἑκάστους πλήθει τῶν στρατιωτῶν καὶ τῶν ὑπάρχων</u> καὶ τροφῆς ἀπείργων καὶ κατακλείων ἠδυνήθη βραδύτερον μὲν ἀκινδυνότερον δὲ κατατρῖψαι καὶ ἐκτρυχῶσαι καὶ ἐκκόψαι αὐτούς.

Cary rendered the Greek "by intercepting small groups, thanks to the number of his soldiers and under-officers." The implication of this would be, that the Roman forces themselves were split up into small task-units under subordinate commanders (ὕπαρχοι) to tackle the large number of fortified points held on the hilltops by relatively small formations of Jewish troops. Whatever the acceptability of Cary's translation in the light of the Greek text, it is appropriate to the tactical reality as I understand it.

As regards the number of strong points and villages, can Dio's figures be relied on? There exists an independent Jewish source, the relevance of which to Dio's text has been recognized by Professor Yeivin,[290] although Buechler long ago noted its relevance to the war: this is <u>Midrash Lamentations,</u>[291] a 3rd-century commentary, where a discussion is reported concerning the number of battles fought by Hadrian; the issue is between 52 and 54. The bearing on Dio's figure is clear; whether or not these scholars had read Dio's unabbreviated text, we may be sure they had their own information. In any case, Dio's number for the Jewish villages captured is a circumstantial figure; Opitz[292] suggested that it was derived from a senatorial resolution honouring Julius Severus; Schürer, for his part, believed that the information came from Hadrian's own autobiography.[293]

Recent archaeological surveys in Judaea may enable a further critical examination of Dio's figure. The following were the results of these surveys, conducted in 1967 and 1968:[294]

		Roman sites	Sq km surveyed	Sq km per site
1.	Judaea (Hebron area)	52	800	16
2.	Benjamin and Mountains of Ephraim	60	1000	16
3.	Ephraim-Menasseh	200	1460	7
4.	Wilderness of Judaea and Central Jordan Valley	133	1400	11

The surveyors of Ephraim-Menasseh themselves stated that there remained additional unrecorded sites in their area. My own visits to the region suggested to me that in some sectors the number of sites could be quadrupled. The relatively high frequency in Ephraim-Menasseh is understandable in view of the fertility of its soils and its abundant water supply. Notable, moreover, is the density of sites in the Wilderness of Judaea and the Central Jordan Valley, most of which area is either waterless or composed of highly salinated soil. While about 30 of the sites here may be subtracted because they are purely military, this alone would lead one to suspect that in Area 2, as in Area 3, further unrecorded sites are to be found. If we double the number of each, a total of 585 is arrived at, giving an average area of 8 sq kilometres per site in Area 2 and 3.5 sq kilometres per site in Area 3. Avi-Yonah, estimating the rural population of the hill country of Western Palestine in the Byzantine period,[294a] arrived at the figure of 1,466,000 over an area of 10,000 sq kilometres. His calculation was based on archaeological surveys of relatively small selected areas. His population figure, however, as it relates to the Byzantine period, must be lowered, since the sites under discussion belong to the Roman period, when they were fewer. In Area 2 the increase in the Byzantine period was nearly 100 percent; in Areas 3 and 4, the figures appear to have remained fairly stationary. In Area 1 the increase was also 100%, and the size of some of the villages increased. This would reduce the total population of the Roman period to some 552,427 souls, and the average per village to 1,241, on the basis of the area surveyed, which covered approximately 4,466 square kilometres. The average population of the present-day Arab village, on the other hand, varies between 500 and 1000; ancient Gezer possessed in the Early Bronze Age, on the lowest estimate of D. Webley,[294b] 1,125 souls, cultivating an area of no more than 3.35 hectares, though with grazing land the total area amounted to 2 square kilometres. The conclusion would seem to be that while the average population-figure per site may be too high, the number of identified settlements is obviously too low. Indeed Dr. Mosheh Kokhbi, the editor of the survey, believes that the percentage of sites still unrecorded is considerable, and that the average area per village-site was considerably less than would appear from the survey. It is further important to remember that the archaeological survey of 1967-8 did not include the area west of the 1967 cease-fire line, or the Jerusalem corridor, which would add a considerable number of sites.

We must conclude provisionally that if the above population figure corresponds fairly well with the number of Jewish casualties reported by Dio (580,000), it does not account for the additional deaths by plague and famine or the large number of prisoners sold into slavery. If however Dio's figure of 985 villages captured appears to be too large, it nevertheless seems highly probable that the revolt was not confined to Judaea, but included Samaria and may well have extended into Lower Galilee as far as the Tzippori-Tiberias line, and have affected Peraea, also Idumaea as far south as the Negev.

THE TACTICAL FACTORS

The tactical picture behind Dio's account is the steady isolation and reduction of numerous village-units and rural centres, whose position in the terrain has been briefly described above. But that was in the sixth phase of the war, when the Jews were on the defensive. What of the earlier phases, which may have involved the capture of Jerusalem, almost certainly the advance to the coast, and possibly the annihilation of XXII Deioteriana?

The only scholar both to have grasped the military reality of the first phase and to have set down his interpretation with terse brevity in print, was the late Dr. Fritz Heichelheim.[294c] The initial Jewish success, he believed, was gained by infiltration between the Roman posts, which so became isolated and were wiped out one by one, following which a ring of fortified villages was established round each. This is of course a back-induction from Dio's account of the sixth phase of the war. So far as the hill country is concerned, it carries conviction; it implies that the Roman posts controlled only the valley-routes, not the hill-villages. As a result of these tactics, the legion X Fretensis at Jerusalem was threatened with isolation, and worse, with annihilation in a defile as it retreated to the maritime plain. Presumably the commander had learned something from the experience of Cestius Gallus, and took care to have with him light-armed troops before the retirement was attempted. The X Fretensis, at any rate, does not vanish from the Roman army list.

This brings us to the question of the annihilation of XXII Deioteriana, and, indeed, to the whole problem of the Jewish occupation of the south and central maritime plain. This phase may have been brief; but it must have involved a collision with legionary forces, whether the VI Ferrata or the legions despatched from Syria and Egypt.[295] It is of course possible that XXII Deioteriana was not wiped out in a single action, but suffered such heavy losses in the course of prolonged operations that it had to be disbanded.[296] This, however, merely poses the tactical problem in another form. It seems to be probable, that the first Roman counterattacks were made on the hill country with insufficient support of mobile auxiliary units. Both in attack and defence, indeed, the Jews may not have forgotten the lessons of the past, and we shall examine the evidence for this in respect of defence shortly. Where attack is concerned, the two instances involving fighting between Jews and Romans which may illustrate what happened under Hadrian, are: a) the killing, by missile-fire, of the centurion and forty men of a Roman centuria surrounded by the followers of the insurgent leader Athrongaeus in 4 BC, during the rising succeeding Herod's death. This took place near Emmaus. The word for "shot down" here is κατηκόντισαν , the weapons used, presumably, javelins.[297] Roman legionaries could be fairly immune to missiles under the protection of their large <u>scuta</u>, especially if formed into close order. But these may have been auxiliary troops. In any case they would have been attacked from ambush, probably from higher ground on the flank, while they were strung out in convoy - for they were convoying corn and weapons. b) The disastrous retreat of Cestius Gallus from Jerusalem.[298] Josephus' account involves grave difficulties from a topographical point of view, and some from a military angle. It is an account of a column in retreat ceaselessly attacked from the rear and from higher ground on each flank. The operative passage is that describing the situation on the road to Beth Horon.[299] "On the open ground their movements were less harassed by the Jews, but once the Romans became involved in the defiles and began the descent, one party of the enemy went ahead of them, and barred their egress, another drove the rearguard down into the ravine, while the main body lined the heights above the narrowest part of the route, and covered the legions with showers of arrows (βέλεσιν). Here, while the infantry were hard put to it to defend themselves, the cavalry were in still greater jeopardy; to advance in order down the road under the hail of darts was impossible, to charge up the slopes was impracticable for horse; on either side were precipices and ravines, down which they slipped and were hurled to destruction... only the intervention of night enabled the Romans to find refuge in Beth Horon."[300]

The inconsistency of the account will be noticed. At first this is an account of a column attacked in a defile; then it becomes a column attacked on a downward slope flanked by cliffs and ravines. In point of fact the Beth Ḥoron route is not a "pass" in any sense; it consistently follows a watershed between two streambeds flowing in deep gorges, possesses excellent flank-command,[301] and only in its most westerly section, where it finally drops to the plain, is it commanded for a very short distance by higher ground on both sides. But this is 3½ kilometres west of Lower Beth Ḥoron. Unless Cestius' force pursued the path in the gorge (Wadi Salmin) to south of the above road - which is improbable - his situation would have been militarily advantageous from the point of view of flank command. It would have been disadvantageous for the use of cavalry, which had no room to deploy. Even on the assumption that the situation was as described by Josephus,[302] one asks why Cestius could not have recovered some advantage by using his archers, of whom he had about 4,700 from Commagene and Emesa, according to Josephus.[303] Nor can the action be understood by reference to Judah the Maccabee's defeat of the Greek force under Seiron in the same sector, in 166/165 BC. This was a success achieved by a well-planned ambush from concealment and a lightning attack at a point flanked on one side by a slope and on the other by a steep drop, and the Greeks were not, apparently, a large force.[304] But these criticisms are beside the point; what is described is a real tactical situation, whereever it actually occurred, which involved the attack on a column from the rear and flanks in a defile. Neither the infantry nor the cavalry can deploy; the archers are either unexploited due to the confusion and lack of ability of the commander, or themselves infected by the general demoralization. For final protection the Roman force has to utilize the defensive capabilities of a Jewish upland village.

The Beth Ḥoron picture, irrespective of its accuracy with regard to Cestius' retreat, is the one which could best explain the predicament of Roman heavy infantry in a Judaean defile, commanded by commanders who had not learned the correct utilization of lightarmed and missile troops, or did not dispose of them, in a mountainous terrain. It would explain the annihilation or attrition of XXII Deioteriana.

Cestius' utilization of Beth Ḥoron village is relevant to the question of Jewish defensive tactics in the second phase of the war. We have referred to the Judaean mountain village as one of the chief elements of Jewish military resistance; the other, according to Dio, was the stronghold. Here again, legitimate analogies may be drawn from the war of 66-73 in order to understand the tactics involved. A case in point is the village of Yapha (Yaphia') which stands at 500 metres above sea-level south-west of Nazareth, and was fortified by Josephus.[305] The village possessed two successive walls; a number of the defenders, who had advanced to meet the Romans outside the village, were trapped between them and slaughtered; the inner wall was then stormed by scaling, but it took the Roman troops six hours' fighting in the narrow streets of the village before the place was finally taken. The total Roman attacking force consisted, according to Josephus,[306] of 3,000 infantry and 1,500 cavalry. The lesson of this operation was less the storming of the fortifications, which was facilitated by the error of the majority of the defenders in making a sortie which ended with their annihilation - than in the difficulty experienced by the attackers in overcoming resistance within the village itself. The alleys of a closely built-up area - especially if they are twisting and tortuous - are a death-trap for infantry, who cannot deploy in them and are exposed to missiles from both sides and above.[307]

If Yapha may serve as a model for the tactical importance of the hill-village as it reappears in the Second Revolt, Gamala may be taken as a forerunner of the fifty strongholds referred to by Dio in the same war.[308] The details of this site and the difficulties faced by Agrippa and Titus in its capture need not be repeated here: almost completely surrounded by ravines, its houses within the walls rose in tiers one above the other, so that each tier commanded the one below it.[309] The first unsuccessful Roman assault became a disaster <u>after</u> the attackers had entered the built-up area.

The Roman forces therefore faced the problem of reducing numerous mountain blocks, isolated by slopes and valleys, and occupied by strong points and fortified villages of the type we have described. They further had to secure themselves against the risks involved in advancing through defiles commanded by higher ground on one or both sides. The obstacles offered by terracing and rockstrewn slopes have been referred to. One further question, however, must be answered, namely, to what extent did woodland and maquis oppose an additional impediment to troop-movements over the mountain-blocks of the area? The question resolves itself into two elements: 1) To what extent is Judaea a naturally wooded region? 2) To what extent may it be visualized as wooded in the 'thirties of the 2nd century of the current era?

L. Rost investigated the existence and extent of ancient woodland in central Judaea; his work was published over forty years ago.[310] By recording isolated trees or small groups of such he was able to determine the limits of the ancient wooded area. These defined an area limited on the west by the meeting of the Cenomannian and Turonian limestones on a line running south from Sh'ar ha-Gai (Bab al-Wad) through Surif and Haras to Beit 'Awa, whence it turned eastward round Hebron and northward along the watershed to Solomon's Pools; here it veered north-west-by-west to Bethar, then due north through Tzobah and Qiriat Ye'arim (Abbu Gosh) to Abbuqash north of Ramallah and on to Qatra ('Atra). The northern extension of the western and eastern limits of the wooded zone are not defined by Rost, who states that on the east it joined the Samaritan forest-area, and that the northern limit was not definable.

The commonest tree surviving in this area was then the oak (Quercus coccifera); after it in order of frequency were the pistachio (Terebinthus palaestina), the carob and the Aleppo pine. An analysis of pollen-specimens in soil taken from a later hellenistic/early Roman stratum within an ancient field-tower near Ḥirbet Tzir, two kilometres north of 'Azzoun (see p. 30), identified oak and juniper.[310a] Vines are attested in the same area by archaeological evidence. The maquis of the same area was composed, in Rost's time, of Quercus coccifera, terebinth and arbutus; the colonizers of cleared areas consisted chiefly of Styrax officinalis (storax), Rhamnus palaestina (buckthorn) and hawthorn; today we should add Poterium spinosum.

In addition to the natural woodland, it must be assumed that the cultivated trees - vines, olives and other fruit-bearers - were not absent from the Judaean landscape.

The woodlands of the Jerusalem district, it must be supposed, had suffered considerable damage during the Jewish war of 66-73. We hear, for instance, of timber for siege-works being brought from a distance of a hundred stadia (about $12\frac{1}{2}$ miles - 20 kilometres) from Jerusalem.[311] Bethar and Tzobah are each eleven kilometres from the old city, which suggests (if Josephus' figures are accurate) that considerable inroads had already been made into the wooded areas. However, assuming a return of fairly normal conditions, recovery of the woodland trees and fruit-plantations would have taken place well before the time of Hadrian. It is authoritatively stated that natural maquis revives in country 250-300 m above sea-level and above, where the annual rainfall is not less than 250-400 mm. The arbutus in good conditions grows to two metres within five to six years, the carob attains the same height within ten years, the Aleppo pine in plantation conditions grows to two metres in four to five years. The oak, on the other hand, takes some 70 years to attain full growth and could not have done so between 70 and 132 but might nevertheless have reached an appreciable height by the latter date. Rost records[312] that he found the oak, terebinth and arbutus in the Judaean area standing to an average height of $1\frac{1}{2}$ to $2\frac{1}{2}$ metres. This being the case, woodland would have been an additional encumbrance to troop-movement, more especially on the lower slopes of the hills, and would have afforded good cover over considerable areas to small bodies of Jewish defenders engaged in ambush, surprise attacks, reconnaissance, escape and concealed movement. Its effect on troop-formations in combat is well illustrated in Tacitus' account of the battle of Bedriacum:[313] et per locos arboribus ac vineis impeditos non una pugnae facies: comminus eminus catervis et cuneis concurrebant. In other words, smaller formations are needed for the work of clearing woodlands of the enemy - especially in broken country. Vespasian's dispositions, as he advanced into Galilee, are instructive:[314]

τοὺς μὲν γε ψιλοὺς τῶν ἐπικούρων καὶ τοξότας προάγειν ἐκέλευσεν, ὡς ἀνακόποιεν τὰς ἐξαπιναίους τῶν πολεμίων ἐπιδρομὰς καὶ διερευνῷεν τὰς ὑπόπτους καὶ λοχᾶσθαι δυναμένους ὕλας.........

The use of archers would have been essential in these circumstances; slingers on the other hand would have been important for advance up terraced slopes and stony broken ground in the more open areas, the more so since the Judaean hill country provides an inexhaustible supply of ready-to-hand ammunition for the slinger, who finds in the country's numerous terraces a first rate position from which to use it in defense.[315]

THE CONTEMPORARY TACTICAL SITUATION IN THE ROMAN ARMY

It is therefore clear that the reduction of the hill country required primarily lightarmed troops operating in comparatively small tactical units, supported by archers and slingers, and comprising a larger number of infantry than cavalry. The latter could operate successfully only in limited areas of the hill country; they would however have been essential for patrolling the communications between the blocks of high ground, for enforcing their isolation from one another, and for preventing infiltration between them.

Before we examine what is known of the actual composition of the forces ultimately brought to bear on the forces of Ben Kosba in the critical stage of the war, it would be as well to discover, in so far as we can, what were the already existent practice and stage of development of the Roman army in the sphere of tactics relating to comparable terrains elsewhere in the Empire, or in general.

Although the fundamental tactics of the Roman army, and the division of function between the legionary infantry and the auxilia, including light infantry, cavalry, and missile-troops, had not changed by the 'thirties of the 2nd century, a number of developments are nevertheless discernible at this time, whose origin is traceable to the encounter with new modes of combat on the part of the enemies whom the Empire now had to face. The most important of these were the Sarmatians, Roxolani and allied peoples on the north-east, and the Parthians, Alans and kindred folk on the east. Both the Sarmatians and the Parthians were skilled as mounted archers, while the Parthians and Roxolani had developed heavily armed cavalry exercizing shock-tactics with the thrust of the long lance (catafractarii). The impact of the latter method of attack is easily seen in the battle formation adopted to face it by Arrian in his encounter with the Alani in AD 134.[316] The influence of heavy cavalry (catafractarii), however, need not concern us here, since the Jews of Judaea did not use them, if, indeed, they used cavalry at all.[317] More important for our theme is the influence of the mounted archers of the Parthians, the Sarmatians and allied peoples; this certainly led, particularly from the time of Trajan, to a considerable increase of archer units in the Roman army, whether mounted or on foot.[318] Archers and slingers were being recruited by Rome as allies from non-Roman peoples in the republican period;[319] under the Empire there were both cohorts and alae of archers, also numeri;[320] the raising of such cohorts had begun under Augustus; a number can be attributed to the Flavian period. At least eight units were raised for Trajan's Dacian and Parthian campaigns; others under Hadrian and Antoninus Pius.[321] Both Cestius Gallus and Vespasian added some thousands of archers to their forces in Judaea, derived from the peoples of local allied potentates (Emesa, Commagene, Agrippa's kingdom, Nabataea).[322] These were not part of the Roman establishment, but allied troops who returned to their countries at the end of hostilities. The survey of Van de Weerd and Lambrechts shows that all the Roman archer troops were recruited from the Orient and Thrace.

This recruitment of archers from allied peoples to corps which did not constitute a permanent part of the military establishment, leads us to consider the numeri.

The origin and development of these units has been a subject of controversy among students of the Roman army ever since Mommsen,[323] who considered them as provincial militias embodied in the imperial army and as one of the factors leading to its barbarization. Vittinghof[324] thought them to have been initially analogous to the auxilia, differing from them only in so far as they continued to be regarded as peregrini. E. Stein[325] on the other hand related them to the provincial militias, minimizing their alleged barbarian character, but admitting their continued inferiority of status. Rowell's evaluation[326] did not materially differ from Stein's. It is generally agreed that the numeri were initially of native, generally of barbarian derivation, operating as light-armed troops and retaining their own languages and modes of fighting; most of them did not attain citizenship on discharge down to the Diocletianic reform. But on their precise tactical significance views have been less clear or decisive. Till recently, the epigraphical evidence was generally accepted to mean that the numeri appeared as organized units officially and permanently incorporated in the Roman military establishment under Hadrian, or, possibly, at earliest, under Trajan.

The latest scholar to devote a study of considerable length to the numeri is H. Callies.[327] Callies holds that the origin of the numeri is among the Hilfskontingenten[328] of non-Roman peoples, recruited for the duration of emergency and only serving under their own commanders. They were raised both from within and from without Roman territory. Like all the Hilfskontingenten, they were enrolled to carry out tactical functions which the legions and auxiliary units were less able to perform. At the end of the Republic and in the earlier Empire there began a gradual assimilation of a number of these units to normal auxilia, in that their service became permanent, and they received Roman officers and organization. But many such bodies continued to be mobilized for limited periods and to serve under their own commanders. Trajan made a very extensive use of Moorish cavalry formations of this type under their leader Lusius Quietus against the Dacians and the Parthians. The use in the orient of considerable numbers of such troops under their own kings, the rulers of allied client states, by Cestius Gallus and Vespasian, has already been mentioned. Arrian used local native levies on a smaller scale against the Alani in 134. In the 2nd century a special type of Hilfskontingent appears, raised from conquered peoples, probably under the terms of peace agreements, and apparently organized in their own units, but not as permanent components of the Roman army. But these units began to serve permanently, often abroad, received Roman officers, and became a permanent element of the forces; such more particularly were the oriental archer battalions of Palmyra.[329]

Under Antoninus the first inscriptions recording numeri appear, in which the term is linked with the names of distinct nationalities (e.g. the Brittones). Epigraphically the term numerus is found earlier, then meaning any military unit, formation or detachment, or a component of a unit. It can also apply earlier, and more particularly later, to a body of troops with a peculiar technical function (singulares, exploratores, frumentarii). The "national" numeri, in Callies' opinion, were only organizationally, not functionally, an innovation; in tactical function they originally differed in no respect from the various Hilfskontingenten raised hitherto and henceforward. The innovation lay in their incorporation in the military establishment, under Roman officers, and often in their allocation to fixed stations. Various units in Dacia and Germany which appear as numeri with distinctive national appellations from the later 2nd century, however, are known earlier under their national appellation only, without the designation of 'numerus', and therefore probably already existed at that time.[330] As such, some can be traced back to Hadrian; but the model for their creation was not, as often thought, Trajan's Moorish levies, thinks Callies, but the Hilfskontingenten which it had been the practice to recruit throughout the principate.

If we accept Callies' view, therefore, are we to conclude that the "national" numeri that emerge in the late 'thirties of the 2nd century do not represent any sort of new need or fresh solution of a tactical requirement? Callies himself devotes a chapter [331] to the reason for the formation of the national numeri. His conclusion is that they originated with Hilfskontingenten whose native tactics were of value against barbarians, serving as light mobile forces against enemies who generally did not give open battle, and whom they countered with their own methods, more especially since the auxilia, also light-armed and of non-Roman derivation, had normally lost their peculiarly native aptitudes in the course of decades of recruitment far from their places of origin.[332]

Since Callies wrote, new evidence has emerged bearing on the date and conditions of the formation of the numeri as permanent and integral units of the Roman army. This was furnished by Baatz's excavation of the Numeruskastell of Hesselbach on the inner German (Odenwald) Limes.[333] The various Brittones or Numeri Brittonum whose inscriptions have been found along this Limes from the reign of Antoninus Pius, occupied a characteristic type of fort whose area averaged 0.6-0.7 hectare approximately. These troops were till recently thought to have come as dediticii from the area of Scotland reoccupied in connection with the erection of the Wall of Pius.[334] But the excavation of the Hesselbach Numeruskastell showed that the fort had been built as early as 95, and although there might have been a change of garrison at the end of Period I in the fort's history, in about 120, there was no change from Period 2 to 3, i.e. from 120 to c. 150, nor does Baatz think it probable that there was a change even in 120. In other words, the numerus may well have arrived in Germany as early as 95, and the transfer is evidently to be associated with the last years of Domitian. As Baatz thought, the move may have been less a consequence of events in Britain than a result of the need to strengthen the Limes in Germania Superior. On the other hand it must be remembered that the new evidence is at present confined to Hesselbach, and cannot therefore be regarded as decisive; it is also possible that the end of Period I represented the arrival of the numerus in the course of a Hadrianic reorganization.

The strength of the numerus at Hesselbach, as established by Baatz, was about 120 men in Period 1, in Period 2, 120 infantry and 20 cavalry (3 centuriae and a turma). This confirms epigraphical evidence from other quarters that the numeri consisted of both horse and foot.[335]

Callies' suggestions concerning the tactical functions of the numeri in Germany are less satisfactory. He thinks [336] that they guarded advanced posts in forested areas difficult of access, where observation was impeded.

He goes on to propose that as inscriptions at several forts (e.g. Welzheim, Obernburg) associate numeri with numeri exploratorum, they would have performed similar scouting duties; the attachment of local placenames to numeri in Germany (generally those of rivers), in Dacia, and in one case in Britain - he interprets to imply duties specific to the areas concerned, e.g. the guarding of the Neckar valley. All this has sense, but does Callies' final conclusion [337] that the function of the numeri was a sort of local defence, for observation, reconnaissance (Aufklärung) and guard, conform with his own view of their original tactical function?

In 81 Domitian opened his campaign against the Chatti of the Wetterau.[338] The tactical requirements of this war were such as to make it very probable that they formed the background for the first organization of the numeri, and would therefore support the earlier date of 95 for their presence on the inner Limes. It has been stated [339] that the Wetterau, which constituted a considerable part of the area overrun by the Roman forces, was, as a local region, not forested;[340] this is confirmed by reference to works of geography. The information provided by Frontinus, who was present at the campaign, must therefore apply to the country to the east and west of the Wetterau. He relates that Domitian "cum subinde Chatti equestre proelio in silvas refugiendo deducerent, iussit suos equites, simulatque ad impedita ventum est, equis desilire pedestrique pugna confligere, quo genere consecutus est, ne quis iam locus victoriam eius moraretur".[341] Here we have the problem of tackling a dangerous rapidly-moving enemy in wooded hill country where cavalry could not penetrate. For the penetration of such a terrain, smaller bodies of infantry and dismounted cavalry were needed. Whatever the outcome of the controversy whether the erection of Domitian's line of watchtowers along the northern slope of the Wetterau preceded or succeeded the capture of the Chattan hillforts,[342] it is clear that in order to occupy the Upper Taunus and Vogelberg it would have been necessary to drive roads through the forest by the creation of cleared rides, to gain control of the region. By Hadrian's time the forts of the Wetterau Limes included a number of Numeruskastellen;[342a] the move of the Odenwald auxiliary units to the new Outer Limes (Miltenberg-Lorch), till recently dated to Pius, may have taken place under Hadrian,[343] and on this stretch also some Numeruskastellen are known between the cohort forts, but they are more numerous on the sector that linked Lorch with the Danube.

Is this new distribution an indication that the numeri now became static police? Several reasons can be advanced against this view. 1) The allocation of such duties would have contradicted the whole function for which these units had existed ever since they were first employed by the Roman army, namely, as mobile troops operating in difficult country and using the combat methods of their barbarian opponents. 2) A number of the forts occupied by the numeri on the Limes - and especially in the Wetterau and in the sectors flanking it on the west and east, were situated on rivers. These were both routes from free Germany into Roman territory and lines of advance into the German area. Not only had they to be blocked, but they offered themselves as routes of advance into hostile territory when an offensive was mounted. 3) Schleiermacher noted that the Wetterau line resembled on a small scale, in respect of the disposition of the forces on it, Trajan's dispositions in Dacia; the Main east of the Wetterau and southward was less a frontier than a strategic line with all the advantages of a navigable river, while the Neckar line could not be regarded as a frontier at all.[344] The implication is that these lines could not be seen as primarily defensive in aim. As to the Outer Limes, its unswerving rectilinear course is in itself evidence that its function was not primarily defensive. 4) Several of the numeri were associated with numeri exploratorum and occupied the same forts with them. Other numeri themselves later developed into numeri exploratorum.[345] This surely signifies that they were primarily mobile units, and remained so. 5) It is agreed by far the majority of scholars that the auxilia garrisoning the Limites of the Empire were not regarded by their commands as the instruments of a primarily defensive policy.[346] Both in Germany and in Dacia most of the numeri are found each to have formed part of a tactical group composed of two or three auxiliary units stationed in its sector.[347] If we take into account the nature of the terrain in either of these countries, it will be clear that when a reconnaissance or sortie was made beyond the frontier, the numerus would be a necessary component of the brigade, especially in wooded or hilly country, scouting ahead and securing the flanks during advance through such regions.[348] 6) The composition of the numeri to include both infantry and cavalry is in favour of this tactical rôle. It also has significance in relation to Judaea, since Vespasian favoured this type of unit. During the Jewish war he established garrisons of this composition at Jaffa, Haditta, Gerasa and Jericho. The garrison of Ascalon in 66 already possessed a like composition; Camp F2 at Masada, occupied 73-111, was garrisoned by four turmae of cavalry and two centuries of infantry, the latter, it seems, legionary.[349] The task performed by the force at Jaffa has some bearing on the tactical purpose of such formations; the infantry held the fort, while the cavalry ravaged the countryside. In other circumstances, we should read for "ravage" - "reconnoitre" or "conduct fighting patrols".[350]

We may sum up the conclusions to be derived from our brief survey of the tactical developments in the Roman army in the period from Domitian to Hadrian. Encounter with the peoples both on the eastern Danube and on the eastern frontier of the Empire led to a considerable development of archer units, whether on foot or mounted. Campaigns in Germany and Dacia created an increased need of mobile light-armed units, both infantry and cavalry, using barbarian modes of combat, for use in broken and forested regions. There was also need of increased light cavalry in the plainland areas of the orient (cf. the use of the Moors of Lusius Quietus in Parthia).

THE TACTICAL COMPOSITION OF THE ROMAN FORCES IN JUDAEA

Of these developments, the most important bearing on the Jewish war of Hadrian are those relating to numeri and to archers. Vespasian and Titus had clearly understood the importance of archers for operations in wooded and mountainous country; they also utilized combined infantry and cavalry contingents for reconnaissance, garrison-duty and aggressive patrol.

For information on the Jewish war of Hadrian's time, we must scrutinize what is known of the composition of the Roman forces commanded by Julius Severus in the final offensive phase of the operations.

The legionary force was exceptionally large, although its exact strength cannot be estimated. The X Fretensis and VI Ferrata were already in the country. The III Gallica may be deduced to have moved to Judaea at the opening of the war from CIG 4033, which records that Tiberius Severus, commander of V Scythica, took over the duties of Publius Marcellus, legate of Syria, when he proceeded to the war, presumably with the other Syrian legion; this is independently proved by two other inscriptions.[350a] XI Claudia sent a vexillation from Moesia Inferior, as shown by an inscription from Bethar;[351] II Traiana, from the same province;[352] probably X Gemina, a vexillation from Pannonia.[353] Legions from other provinces were: XXII Deioteriana, from Egypt (see above); III Cyrenaica, probably from Arabia;[354] XII Fulminata, from Cappadocia.[355] The rock inscription at Bethar,[355a] recording the legions I Italica (vexillation, Moesia Inferior), V Macedonica (Moesia Inferior, vexillation), and XI Claudia (Vexillatio - above), appears to record a command in Judaea in XI Claudia only, but the presence of V Macedonica is independently evidenced by an epitaph from Shechem,[356] so that by inference a vexillation of I Italica was also in Judaea. The minimum number of troops represented by these three vexillations, recorded in the Bethar inscription, is perhaps to be calculated from the large camp south of the fortress, which possessed an area of 32 hectares (80 acres); this area was sufficient to contain at least 9,000 men, but in field-conditions could have held more. Strong vexillations are therefore indicated.[356a]

More problematic is the number of auxiliary units participating in the war. A number of units can be listed whose participation may be considered probable: their actual presence can be satisfactorily proved only in a few cases. Nor does the total number arrived at as probable necessarily correspond to the forces really in action. Consequently any conclusions must be tentative.

The auxiliary units which may have been in action in Judaea can be divided into several groups according to the type of evidence pointing to the possibility of their presence.

1. The units recorded in Judaea by Diploma XIV of AD 86.[357]
2. The units stationed in Judaea in AD 139 according to Diploma CIX.[358]
3. Units transferred from Raetia to Judaea for the war, as established by the enquiries of Professor A. Radnóti.[359]
4. Two Danubian units believed by Wagner to have participated in the war.[360]
5. Units known to have participated on various other epigraphical evidence.[361]

The auxiliary cohorts and auxilia concerned are listed, together with the epigraphical evidence for their conclusion, in an appendix to the present work.(P.63).

The grand total of the above troops amounts to no more than 15,904 men, without reckoning a vexillation of unknown strength from Pannonia[362] recorded at Samaria[363] and a contingent of praetorians that probably accompanied Hadrian in the field (J.R.S. IV, 1914, pp. 13-16). As seven complete legions appear to have been in action in the later phase of the war, besides vexillations from four other legions, of unknown strength,[364] at least 42,000 legionaries must have been on active service in Judaea, implying, one would suppose, at least an equal number of auxiliary troops. On this estimate, it is clear that the above number of auxilia, reckoned on the evidence of the "probables", is less than half the actual number in the field. It may nevertheless be worthwhile analysing the composition of these troops, always bearing in mind that any conclusions rest on a tentative basis.

Q = quingenariae   E = equitatae   M = miliariae   S = sagittariorum

Alae	Q	7	3,696		
	QS	1	528	4,224	
Cohortes	Q	14	6,720		
	QE	4	2,000		
	M	2	2,000		
	QS	2	960	11,680	Total 15,904

Grouped in tactical units:

Archers

Cohortes	QS	2	960	
Alae	QS	1	528	1,488

Infantry

Cohortes	Q	14	6,720	
	M	2	2,000	
	QE	4	2,000	minus cavalry (480)
				10,240

Cavalry

Alae	Q	7	3,696	
Alae	QS	1	528	
Cohortes (cavalry only)	QE	4	480	4,704

Several points call for comment. There is a total of 22 infantry units as against eight cavalry units. There is as yet no record of an <u>ala miliaria</u>; as such <u>alae</u> were the flower of the cavalry,[365] and ranked senior in the army-list, evidently, at least according to our present information, this arm was not regarded as of primary importance in the Jewish campaign. But four infantry units were <u>equitatae</u>, bringing the number of mounted men in the field up to 4,704. This figure might give some support to our previous observation of the favour with which mixed formations of infantry and cavalry were regarded in the conditions of Judaea. The archer units compose no more than 10% of the recorded forces, and one would expect a stronger representation. It can only be commented, that two strong archer cohorts were in Syria in 157, both <u>miliariae</u>, and one had certainly been in the east since Trajan's time; these were the I Ulpia and V Ulpia Petraeorum. These may have been among the forces engaged in Judaea under Hadrian, but there is as yet no evidence to that effect; it is moreover possible that the IV and VI Petraeorum, both in Judaea in 139, were archer units. Their presence would have brought the percentage of archers among the known units up to 14%. Generally the above composition may be claimed, within the limits of our knowledge, to respond to the tactical requirements of the war-theatre as we have endeavoured to define them.[366]

Two questions, however, will at once occur to the critical reader: why such a massive legionary force, and where are the numeri, whose tactical capabilities we have conceived as so well adapted to the problems created by Hadrian's Jewish War?

It is not easy to give a satisfactory explanation for the very large legionary concentration. The geographical positions occupied by the legions during the war, on epigraphical evidence, do not tell us enough of their movements, nor can all the known legionary inscriptions be dated with complete confidence to Hadrian's time. It may however be noted that a number of these inscriptions are located round the edge of the area of hostilities in so far as we can define it; Gadara, Tell Shalem south-east of Beth Shean, Beth Shean itself, Tiberias, Samaria, Shechem, Beth Govrin. The Bethar rock-inscription, recording three legionary vexillations, is obviously connected with the siege of that fortress late in the war; one inscription from Jerusalem, discussed above, may have been set up to commemorate a casualty incurred during operations there. As regards the peripheral legionary records, (excluding a number at Caesarea, obviously the rear headquarters for all operations), they are probably to be interpreted as marking winter-stations. But the military significance of Tiberias in the context of the war has already been suggested, and its function as the end of a patrolled line might indicate that the other peripheral legionary stations were part of an iron cordon drawn round the enemy area. But they also may have marked strategical points of departure for the offensive against an enemy that disposed of interior lines. Gadara, Scythopolis, Samaria and Shechem all occupy points from which advance was easy to the central watershed route connecting Jenin with Jerusalem.[367] Tell Shalem (above p. 30) was placed to block the Jordan Valley southward and to act as a base for attack in that direction. Beth Govrin lay at a point on the military road, built during the war, which describes a circle about Bethar by way of Hebron, Jerusalem and Emmaus.

The legions, clearly, were the main agents which cleared the maritime plain and the valleys of the Jewish forces. But for all the tactical features special to the hill country and requiring first and foremost the presence of lightarmed troops, the legions had a part to play here also. Once the wooded hill country had been penetrated and held, and the lightarmed troops had driven back the resistance and closed in on the fortified centres, the legionaries could advance and deliver the final assault in conditions where their weight and armour counted. The legionary artillery and siege-equipment, once manhandled up the rough terrain - no light task - were needed to prepare the way for this last stage.[367a] Yet even here the legionaries needed the support of lightarmed and missile troops to secure them once they had entered the built-up areas of the villages.[368]

The problem of the numeri is somewhat more obscure. There is at present only one inscription known to me evidencing the presence of numeri in the country, this being from Shechem; it records an eques numerorum Maurorum.[369] This has been ascribed to the civil war between Severus and Pescennius Niger, but it is much more likely to belong to the time of Trajan, when Lusius Quietus brought his Moorish cavalry into Judaea (116-117.) In any case, the term numeri as applied to the Moors, then denoted, it would

47

appear, a large force of non-Roman allied tribes commanded by their own leader (<u>Mauri</u> <u>gentiles</u>). It is not evident that any of these Moorish units were numeri in the sense of regular units officered by Roman officers, till the Antonine period.[370] Hadrian removed Lusius' cavalry from Judaea, hence the connection of the Shechem inscription with the Jewish war of 132, if a possibility, is a remote one.

We cannot of course be certain that no "national" <u>numeri</u> were in Judaea under Hadrian, since few such units put up inscriptions till the end of the 2nd century. It may be noted that of the three Roman forts found along the Beth Govrin-Bethlehem road south of Bethar, Site 16 (0.2 hectares) appears to have accommodation for about 120 men; Site 26 covered 0.4 hectares; both might therefore have housed <u>numeri</u>. Two facts are indeed suggestive; the earliest known <u>numerus</u> in Dacia, recorded in 137, is one of Suri saggitarii;[371] and it may not be a coincidence that the Tiberias-Sepphoris road, with its <u>burgi</u>, was paved in the same year, and that a <u>numerus burgariorum et veredariorum</u> is found on the Red Tower Pass in Dacia Inferior in 138.[372] Yet from these suggestive fragments of information no final conclusion can be drawn. On present evidence, even if the <u>numeri</u> originated as a permanent arm of the Roman forces as early as Domitian's time, they cannot be proved to have operated in Judaea under Hadrian. Apart from the Suri saggitarii, a <u>numerus Raetorum gaesatorum</u> was also raised and fought in Dacia under Hadrian. The gentile name of the widow of a soldier of the numerus exploratorum Germaniciorum, (Ulpia),[373] suggests that this unit was formed early in his reign; this is, of course, a "technical" <u>numerus</u>, but the undoubted association with, or development into, <u>exploratores</u>, of some permanent <u>numeri</u>, must not be forgotten. It would appear, therefore, that there is little information on <u>numeri</u> in the eastern provinces at this time (if we exclude the <u>numeri</u> of Palmyrene archers, a special category) till the end of Hadrian's reign, and we are forced to assume that the tactical functions they were evolved to perform in this period, were carried out in Judaea by the auxilia. It may indeed be conceived that the experiences in Judaea gave an impulse to the development and increase of <u>numeri</u> and <u>numeri exploratorum</u> in other provinces, the more so since we have seen the probability that Roman reconnaissance in Judaea had proved defective at the beginning of the war.

One item of epigraphical evidence, indeed, may be interpreted to support the suggestion that auxiliary troops at this time were performing in Judaea the tasks better suited to <u>numeri</u>. This is an inscription recording the career of M. Statius Priscus, tribune of legion III Gallica and prefect of the cohort IV Lingonum equitata, "vexillo militari donato a divo Hadriano in expeditione Iudaica."[374] It has been supposed that Statius took the vexillation to Judaea as tribune of III Gallica, but Miltner[375] has pointed out that his decoration is hardly appropriate to a legionary officer, hence it is more likely that it was part of the Cohors IV Lingonum that Statius took to the Jewish war, very probably (as Miltner suggests) in connection with Julius Severus' move from Britain, where he was governor, to take command in Judaea.

Why should part of this auxiliary cohort have been despatched so far for the purpose of a campaign the other end of the Empire? My suggestion is that this was one of the British units with special experience in tough hill-fighting; in AD 103, according to a diploma, it was in south Wales,[376] which offered plenty of scope for such operations; its men came originally from the Langres district of France, which was far from flat. Saxer cites a similar case - the transfer of a vexillation of Cohors I Tungrorum miliaria, stationed at Housesteads on Hadrian's Wall, to Noricum in Hadrian's time.[377] I would therefore like to believe that the vexillation of IV Lingonum accompanied Julius Severus to Judaea as a demonstration detachment in order to assist in the training of other auxiliary units engaged in the war in the tactics of hill-fighting.

JUDAEA AND WALES: A COMPARISON

Before we turn to the final phase of the war, it might be instructive to compare Roman military policy in Judaea, as evidenced during the Second Revolt, with that in another region of the Empire not dissimilar in size and structure: I refer to Wales. The size of Wales[*] is not vastly less than that of Judaea west of Jordan, including Galilee; the two countries resemble each other in that both are occupied over the greater part of their areas by mountains, the plainlands being restricted to the coast or to limited inland areas, generally river valleys. Glamorgan very much resembles Galilee in its closely set parallel valleys which are an obstacle to transverse traffic. The most prominent differences are, in Wales, the absence of an important urban focus in the central massif corresponding to Jerusalem, and the numerous river valleys which render penetration of the mountainous districts rather easier than it generally is in Judaea. Further, Wales is approachable from the sea on three sides, and has numerous convenient natural harbours. Various other geographical and economic differences could be noted, but need not be laboured; the extensive hill country and restricted plains present a fundamentally similar strategical problem to the would-be conqueror. The most important difference from Judaea is economic rather than morphological, to wit, that Judaea supported a much more numerous population.

This fact notwithstanding, Rome down to the earlier 2nd century required to hold Wales two legions and an auxiliary force of some 8,500 men in the Caerleon command, and 8,350 in the northern, although several units of the latter (the Chester command) were stationed in the Pennines.[378] Jarrett estimates that at least 5,000 of them were in Wales,[379] so that the auxiliary units there totalled some 13,500 men, and with the legions neared 25,500, always remembering that the XX Valeria Victrix also faced north and northeast, surveying the Lancashire plain, the western Pennines and the Peak District. For comparative purposes, a figure of 22,500 might be adopted. The suppression of the Judaean revolt required seven full legions (42,000 men), and four legionary vexillations numbering not less than 9,000 men and probably more. A total of over 51,000 heavy infantry is thus reached; with auxiliary troops, infantry and cavalry, at least 74,000 troops were engaged (see pp. 44-46). As legionaries generally operated with a force of auxiliary troops at least equal to their own, the above is probably an underestimate.

What are we to conclude from the comparison? To answer this question, we have first to answer several others: how did the Roman army control Wales; did it, or did it not, create a solitude and call it a peace; and if not,

---

[*] See Map 2, p.100.

what, in pari materia, was the relation between the military system and the population? Despite the diligent enquiries of several generations of archaeologists, we do not yet know enough to answer all these questions with certainty, and much is disputed. Nevertheless it is worth venturing a provisional answer by the utilization of the work of Nash-Williams, Jarrett, Grace Simpson,[379b] Foster, Hogg,[379c] Gresham[379d] and Richmond.[379e]

In 110 the military occupation still existed at full strength as outlined above.[380] (See Fig. 2.) It has gaps: no certain Roman fort or camp is yet known in Pembrokeshire, despite a high percentage of smaller native hillforts and enclosures, and one suspects that this region was anticipating its later history as an area ready to collaborate with conquerors and colonizers from outside.[381] Flintshire and Denbighshire (the Deceangli) are curiously empty of forts, in contrast to five hillforts with early Roman material and two with evidence of slighting, presumably by Roman action. A relative absence of occupation in the north-centre, the country of the Ordovices (Dee-Dyfi) is perhaps to be explained by the near-extermination of the tribe;[382] but known hillforts and other earthworks here are few;[383] enquiry in this region has perhaps been inadequate. Anglesey, the original centre of the Druids, is free of forts (excepting the late defended harbour at Caergybi, Holyhead) - suggesting extermination and perhaps partial resettlement. Successful pacification may be argued for the Deceangli and the Demetae latest by the middle years of the 2nd century.

But what of the relation of the forts of the period of Trajan to the population-centres? If we look at these posts in relation to the known areas of hillforts and lesser enclosures, irrespective of period (not enough is known to distinguish the individual periods of most of them - we utilize them here as indicators of habitable areas in the conditions of the time) we can distinguish a) forts that bear an obvious relation to such areas, and b) others that do not. To group a) belong Trawscoed and Llanio, Usk, Brecon, Penygaer, Abergavenny, Caersws, Forden Gaer, Castell Collen, Lloughor, Caerhyn. Pen Llystin and Caernarvon. Group b) includes Pennal, Bryn-y-Gefeiliau, Caergai and Caerau.[384] Tomen-y-mur stands in close proximity to the hillfort of Trawsfynnydd, where Early Iron Age metalwork of the later phase has been found;[385] this is an isolated stronghold, evidently a trouble-centre, and its presence implies a populated area to be identified (at least topographically) with the group of enclosed homesteads shown on C. Gresham's map of these to south-west towards Harlech.[386] It is notable that four forts of group a) - Forden, Brecon, Caerhyn and Caernarvon, are thought by Simpson[387] to have been damaged or destroyed in the middle or end of the 2nd century. Of the forts thought to have been rebuilt in the Antonine period, six belong to group a), two to group b).

A closer scrutiny of the relation between forts and population is made possible for north-western Wales by the use of Gresham's maps of enclosed and unenclosed homesteads in that area.[388] Here again, the homesteads are not necessarily assumed to belong to a defined ancient period - they are merely taken as evidence of areas habitable under ancient conditions. The relation of Caernarvon to the group of enclosed homesteads stretching eastward along the coastal plain to the Conway estuary is here evident; the connection of Tomen-y-Mur with similar sites to south-west has been referred to. Pen Llystin can be related to some enclosed homesteads in its vicinity, but more important are the numerous concentrated unenclosed groups to north and east. The situation of Caerhyn is not clarified by Gresham's maps, but Hogg[389] records a considerable group of hut-sites immediately to its west, the eastern outliers of the coastal settlements extending from Caernarvon. Bryn-y-Gefeiliau, on the other hand, appears to be related to neither type of settlement. On present evidence, it is essentially a communication fort. Those of the huts and hut-groups recorded by Gresham and Hogg which have been excavated have yielded material dating between the 2nd and the late 4th centuries; one (Pant-y-Saer) originated in the pre-Roman period.[390]

It is therefore clear that the castella of Wales in the period of maximum garrisoning fall into two groups, namely, those which watched definable areas of population, and those whose function appears to have been mainly strategical and for the protection of communications. But those that can be related to identifiable areas of contemporary occupation would seem to furnish proof that the population was not exterminated or forcibly removed - though this fate may have befallen the Ordovices. The natives' survival is not contradicted by the fact that by 170 only seven Welsh forts (not including Chester and Caerleon) are known to have been occupied; five more may have been.[391] To the first group belonged Caernarvon (a), Caerhyn (a), Bryn-y-Gefeiliau (b), Forden (a), Caersws (a), Leintwardine and Castell Collen (a); to the second, Llanio (a), Brecon (a), Abergavenny (a), and Gellygaer. Granted that the population was reinforced during the period of Roman rule by external elements from the rest of the province, from Ireland,[392] perhaps from northern Britain, and possibly from elsewhere, it is nevertheless evident that the original inhabitants remained in some strength; when Ptolemy recorded the names of their civitates, he presumably was not merely antiquarianizing,[393] and whatever the scale or significance of the reoccupation of hillforts in the 3rd and 4th centuries, at some (Dinorben, Breiddin, Llanmelin) it was considerable.[394] In the 4th century the Cornovii were strong enough to furnish a fighting unit to the provincial army;[395] they and other civitates ultimately colonized Brittany.[396]

Grace Simpson has concluded that under Hadrian the Roman forces in Britain were inadequate to garrison all the forts of the province known then to have been held, without a division of units.[397] The damage to Welsh forts in the later 2nd century, moreover, shows that the Britons there had not accepted Roman rule or civilization.[398] Generally, however, the Welsh population was not exterminated or deported; the forts were placed at the edge of the occupation areas to watch them, and the military roads were primarily to link the garrisons. The system, with its 13,000 auxiliary troops, could contain the inhabited areas on Hogg's estimate of the population of the northwest, the total cannot have been large, and hardly exceeded 50,000 - but could not do more without the intervention of the two legions stationed to support them from rear stations. The need of seven legions, four legionary vexillations and the corresponding auxilia in Judaea, a territory almost equal to Wales. arose primarily from the former's much larger population.[399] But the garrison that had contained it before the rebellion comprised two legions and about 14,000 auxilia, much as did the contemporary garrison of Wales, and it is to be assumed that in Judaea as in Wales the auxilia were regarded as sufficient for routine police duties, while the two legions were intended to be adequate in the event of revolt. If Simpson's estimate of the situation in Wales is correct, that its native population continued to be a threat despite repression, it is necessary to deduce that it was never exterminated. The continuous pressure of the Pictish tribes and the persistent risings of the Brigantes in the 2nd century, as well as the periodical reduction of the forces for needs in Europe, all lent support to Welsh intransigency. The differentia between the strength of the forces in Judaea in 130 and their strength in 135, therefore, is a tangible expression of the decision of the Roman government to exterminate the Jewish population of the Judaean massif; it was the physical result of the administrative decisions to prohibit circumcision and to set up Aelia Capitolina as the centre of a pagan Judaea. But if this is the conclusion that forces itself upon the investigator, why, despite the virtual emptying of Judaea of its Jewish inhabitants,[400] did two legions remain in the country till late in the 3rd century? VI Ferrata, which then left the province, had watched Galilee, where a Jewish population survived. X Fretensis was then moved south to 'Aqaba to face an external enemy, the nomadic tribes of Arabia. But its base till then, Aelia, had been directed to watching the Wilderness of Judaea, which, as we shall see, retained dissident elements well into the 4th century. If the Jews remained quiet till the 4th century (a clash with the Samaritans is recorded under Severus, but the whole incident is extremely doubtful)[401] the reason was simple - the virtual extermination of the Jewish population of Judaea, the selling into slavery of survivors, and the emigration of the rest from the Judaean highlands to the Greek cities, to Galilee, to other provinces of the Empire, and to Parthian territory (Babylonia).

THE FINAL PHASE

The seventh phase of the war, as suggested above, was the siege and capture of Bethar. The position of Bethar, a few miles west of Jerusalem, suggests that the area originally controlled by Ben Kosba's forces extended very much westward of Jerusalem. The new archaeological features detected and observed in the immediate vicinity of Bethar [402] further suggest that the countryside was still far from clear of insurgent forces when the investment of the fortress was undertaken. Thus quite apart from the two Roman camps (Site 9) now known to lie immediately south of it - the westerly 32 hectares, the easterly 2.4 hectares in extent - at least three Roman posts (nos. 16, 23, 26) lay along the road connecting Beth Govrin with Bethlehem to south of Bethar. Clearly then, the besieging force had to guard against the movement of enemy groups still at large and doubtless based, at least in part, on the Wilderness of Judaea. Two of these sites constitute, so far as I am aware, something new in Roman fortifications in the Near East, at least in the 2nd century. The first, Ḥirbet Um Qa'lah (Site no. 16), is a roughly rectangular structure measuring 15 m by 35 m average width, its long axis lying due east-west. It covers some 0.15 hectares, and is closely packed with barrack buildings, disposed, with the headquarters block, to leave a main street along the long axis and a cross-street somewhat east of the halfway north-south dissection. The headquarters building faces eastward onto the latter street and abuts on the south wall of the fort. The enclosure had three narrow gates, two in the north and south walls respectively, the third in the east wall; the east flank of the enclosure was protected by two detached square towers, and to its east, the other near the north-east corner. The barrack-blocks appear to have accommodated, in all, some 120 men, which would be the equivalent of a numerus, unless the relatively large principia is taken to mean that this was the headquarters of a larger unit half of which was engaged in standing or mobile patrol in the field, from which it was periodically relieved by the other half, using the fort as a place of rest. The relatively small area and close-packed structures of Ḥirbet Um Qa'lah suggest an active and aggressive enemy against whom a maximum of alertness was necessary.

Not dissimilar is Hirbet Kabar (Site 26) further east towards Bethlehem. This is a rather larger enclosure, situated on a spur commanding the road-junction where the highroad from Hebron joined that from Beth Govrin to Bethlehem. The area of the fort is 0.4 ha. i.e. 80 x 50 m, the long axis being orientated rather west of north-south. There is a gate in the east side. The interior structures are only partly traceable, hence no precise estimate of the strength of the garrison can be made, but the buildings were closely packed as at Ḥirbet el-Qa'lah, and the principia probably abutted upon the centre of the west wall. Fundamentally this fort belongs to the same type as that at Site 16. It may be conjectured that its garrison was in the region of 240 men (three centuries).

The fall of Bethar did not end Jewish resistance. The last phase of resistance in the caves of the Wilderness of Judaea is well-known to the scholarly world; less well-known, perhaps, is the evidence for the prolonged and elaborate effort invested by the Roman forces in that region in order to extinguish the last embers of revolt. These installations have recently been surveyed and largely recorded, but not studied or published in very great detail. A general impression of this evidence may be gained from the words of Pesaḥ Bar-Adon, who was responsible for the archaeological survey in the Wilderness of Judaea carried out by the Society for the Archaeological Survey of Israel in 1967 and 1968.[403]

"It would appear that the lines of the fortifications and roads in the Wilderness of Judaea followed those of their hitherto unknown Israelite forerunners. The Romans added military camps, fortifications and forts to the Israelite structures, also utilizing those existing either in their original or in a modified form, since they yield remains of both periods.

"Interesting are the finds in the settlements consisting of houses of dry masonry, the walls of which survive to 1.5-2 metres. The rooms contained sinks and shelves serving as benches or beds, also niches for use as cupboards. Such were found over Naḥal Arugot in the vicinity of 'Ein Geddi....

"Some forty complete rooms were counted in these houses, apart from rooms and dwellings which had been destroyed. The Wadi contained caves adapted as cisterns; steps and a revetted stone path led down to the springs below, similar being found north of Wadi Murabba'at and also where it joins Wadi an-Nar. Here too were remains of structures, steps and a made path leading to water. Inhabited caves were situated near them. The principal finds in all of them were of the Roman period, although they were also used in the Byzantine period.

"It is clear that these structures were built as temporary dwellings by people who had been forced to come here, whether as rebels or as refugees, according to all available data, in the period of Bar Kokhba...

"The survey reveals a clear picture of the entire vast effort invested by the Roman administration and its legions in road-making and in the erection of military camps, fortifications and forts in the desert, and over the entrances and exits of the wadis, in order to block the paths used by the stubborn fighters for liberty, to keep them under siege and to reduce them by cutting them off from their centres and sources in the rear."

The identifiable Roman military structures in this area may be classified, to judge from the publication, into forts and fortlets, blockhouses, signal towers, and roads. The term "forts" here also includes stone-built enclosures which do not contain, so far as can be seen, internal buildings, or only a few, but are equipped with one or more wall-towers that suggest something more than mere marching camps. It also relates to fortified enclosures of Israelite origin reused, according to the finds, in the Roman period. Examples of the last type are Rujum el-Hamiri (Site 230) and Um ez-Zuweitimeh (Site 154).

The forts and fortlets are generally rectangular, frequently with one or more sides set obliquely to the rest. Some appear to be without towers. Unusual is Gasr er-Rabai' (Site 110), a long rectangle divided into two by an internal wall, with a rectangular room (a tower?) abutting on one corner. Its area (1.17 dunams) is exceptional, as most of the forts and fortlets cover between 0.26 and 0.6 dunams; Rujum el-Qat (no. 79) covers one dunam. Two of the forts are simple rectangles.

The blockhouses (Sites 79, 104, 112, 169) vary in size from 8 by 10 to 12 by 12 m; all but one (no. 112) are square; all except no. 112 are subdivided into rooms at ground-level. Nos. 104 and 112 each contains a row of internal piers for supporting a second floor; both have attached enclosures. The three known signal-towers are all square, respectively 6.3 x 3.9; 4 x 3.5 and 7 x 7m in area. That at Site 172 is interesting as it stands within an irregular rhomboidal fenced enclosure measuring approximately 15 x 20 m. Another such tower, rectangular in plan (2 x 1.5 m) farther north in the Jordan Valley (Site 18, Wadi Sa'ad) is surrounded by a circular fence, thus resembling signal-towers known on the German Limes and illustrated on Trajan's Column.[403b] A tower of this sort appears to be referred to in a talmudic passage [404] as a "fenced enclosure and burganin within it."

Two main north-south roads are identified as constituting fortified lines designed to shut in the region occupied by the Jewish insurgents to the east; both extend southward from Bethlehem, the westerly going by Hebron to Carmel and continuing, presumably, to Moleatha (Tell el-Milik). Its course is marked by a blockhouse (Site 79) north of Hebron, and presumably other such structures await discovery. The more easterly road connects Hebron with Teqoa', and crossing the first north of Carmel reaches Yuta, where a third east-west route crossed from Beth Govrin, guarded by a blockhouse (no. 169) several miles north-west of Yuta. The easterly north-south road is guarded by blockhouses (Sites 104, 112) south of Teqoa', and by the fortlet of Ras Jingis (Site 120). Both blockhouses watch points where paths from the Judaean Wilderness to eastward fall into the main north-south highway.

A main route of penetration into the hostile area appears to leave Teqoa' for the south-east, reaching 'Ein Geddi by Naḥal Arugot. The line is watched by camps at 142, a watchtower at 144; a fort and tower at 146, a fort at 148, and a fort and a tower at 154. Further south a fenced signal station is found at 172. A second line of penetration may have been the route southward from Jericho by al-Baqia' parallel with the west shore of the Dead Sea; it turned westward over the 'Arab et-Ta'mirah to reach Herodium. This line is marked by numerous ancient sites recorded by the Israel Survey, but Roman material does not seem to have been observed along it.

Further east along the scarp dropping to the Dead Sea, a network of engineered Roman roads had been found and mapped prior to the present survey; these routes were evidently made or adapted from existing Israelite roads, to enable troop-movement during the reduction of the last centres of resistance.[405] 'Ein Geddi may be assumed to have served as an advanced base at this stage, and with the investment from the east should doubtless be connected the evidence for the presence of a Jewish post at Ḥirbet Qumran during the war.[406]

The small size of the known forts - none exceeds 1.17 dunam in area - suggests that the number of troops engaged in these operations was not very large, and most would have been auxilia.[407] The Naḥal Ḥever camp held about a century, and the division of the fort at Site 52 into two parts by a partition wall, may indicate the presence of two types of troops, one legionary.[407a] Many more troops however must have been necessary to build the various fortifications and roads required for the final suppression of resistance. Furthermore, rear bases would have been necessary for rest, supply, relief and reinforcement in case of need. The known roads point to the possibility that such existed at Bethlehem, Hebron and Carmel, while 'Ein Geddi and Jericho offer themselves as natural bases on the east fringe of the area. There may be confirmation of some of these bases in Jewish scholarly tradition. Midrash Lamentations Rabba (I, 16) states that Hadrian placed forts at Bethel (textual variants are Bethel Yehud and Bethlehem), Kefar Leqitya and Ḥamat. For some time the tendency of scholars was to identify these with Bethel, Kefar Liqia and Emmaus (Ḥamata). This is a logical identification, since these three points are connected by an ancient road traversing high ground north of the present main road from Emmaus (Latrun) to Jerusalem, north of which it joined the watershed road at Bethel. This route possessed considerable tactical command and would have been an effective patrol line shutting in Bethar from the north. Recently, however, in conformity with his minimalist view, Förster has suggested that the three points of Midrash Lamentations should be placed in or near the Wilderness of Judaea and that instead of Bethel, Bethlehem should be read, Kefar Leqitya being (on Förster's suggestion) Ḥirbet el-Qatt (Site 79 of the Israel Survey), between Bethlehem and Hebron. If this is right, then Ḥamat might be the place of that name referred to as "the plain of Tzilan of Ḥamat in Judaea" in the context of the Plain of Tzoar at the south end of the Dead Sea.[408] There are several hot springs (Ḥamot) on the south-west shore of the Sea, and Roman forts near two, viz. 'Ein Boqeq and Zohar. 'Ein Boqeq is post-Diocletianic;[409] the history of Zohar is at present unknown.

The final phase of the struggle was doubtless exceptionally ruthless: the struggle between a soldiery rendered savage by boredom and hardship, and the last remnants of a people for whom liberty was a divine commandment. The mountain road-system enabled the investment to be pushed relentlessly to the very gorges where the last resisters had their caves.[410] Not all of them died by the sword; hunger ended the lives of those whom the military failed to reach.[411] Some groups escaped and survived. (See below).

There is another passage in Midrash Lamentations,[412] which follows immediately on the mention of Hadrian's three forts - the well-known passage listing "pairs" of towns one of which harassed the other. It says: "God commanded Jacob that his enemies should be about him: such are Ḥalmish to Neveh, Qastra to Haifa, Susita to Tiberias, Jericho to Na'aran, and Lydda to Onno." The last pair may be taken to date the list not earlier than the 3rd century, when Onno became a municipality.[413] Qastra, near Haifa, is probably the fort found recently at Sycaminum (p. 29), occupied from Hadrian's time to the 3rd century, and the same may well apply to all the other places named first in the pairs, which are likely enough to have been forts also. We have referred above to the stationing of a quaestionarius of the III Cyrenaica at Ḥalmish (Sur or Basir). The suggested period of these posts would not be contradicted by their absence from the Notitia Dignitatum Orientis,[413a] with the exception of Jericho. If there were forts at the above places, it is probable that those at Sycaminum, Sur, Susita,[414] Lydda and Jericho existed under Hadrian, and with the possible exception of Neveh, marked the extreme limits of Jewish disaffection. In addition, Tosefta[415] refers to a Qastra in Har ha-Melekh.

It is nevertheless not impossible that Jewish activist elements hung on for many years after 135 in the Desert of Judaea. Some of the finds in the caves are much later than that date.[416] The Augustan History[417] records that Antoninus Pius "Iudaeos rebellantes contudit per praesides ac legatos". Eutychius[418] wrote that Jews took refuge from the Roman victory in Syria, Egypt, in the mountains and in the Ghore (et in montes et in regionem Algaur) i.e. in the Jordan Rift, which is likely enough to have included the west side of the Dead Sea, i.e. the Judaean Wilderness. The identification of Ghor with Zoara, the modern es-Safi, at the southern end of the Dead Sea, with a Jewish population before the later 2nd century[418a] and a Roman garrison in the 4th,[419] need not exclude "et in montes". Furthermore it should be noted that even in the 4th century the Limes Palaestinae threw off a spur northward from Moleatha (Tell el-Milik) to include the fort of Chermela (Carmel, al-Kurmel) held by the Equites scutarii Illyriciani.[420] This watershed line continued to watch the Judaean wilderness as it had done under Hadrian.[421]

GENTILE PARTICIPATION?

A point which has not, to the best of my knowledge, been discussed in print is the problem of non-Jewish participation in the war of 132-135. Dio writes:[422]

ἐνεδείκνυντο πολλοί τε ᾽ἄλλοι καὶ τῶν ἀλλοφύλων ἐπιθυμίᾳ κέρδους σφίσι συνελαμβάνοντο καὶ πάσης ὡς εἰπεῖν κινουμένης ἐπὶ τούτῳ τῆς οἰκουμένης κτλ.

There is no evidence of any serious disturbance in the Empire outside Judaea at the time of the revolt, if we exclude the probable pressure on Hadrian's north British frontier which led, early in the following reign, to the reoccupation of the Scottish Lowlands and the building of the Forth-Clyde limes.[423] In consequence we may confine our observations to the near eastern provinces.

It has already been noted (p. 6) that Hadrian's relations with the city of Antioch, according to the Historia Augusta,[424] were bad to the point of hostility. The evidence of the Augustan History, however, is here of very doubtful value. It is rejected by Downey [424a] and Magie,[425] and runs counter to the evidence of Hadrian's own benefactions to the city. Magie[426] thinks that the statement in the History is a distortion of the fact that Hadrian raised Tyre, Damascus and Samosata to metropolitan status equal with that of Antioch itself.[427] One might add that the report could have been influenced by the record of subsequent events under Severus.[428] Nevertheless Antioch, like Alexandria and even occasionally Athens, was, as an ex-capital, apt to be refractory, and there may have been other Greek towns that were prepared to dispute the Emperor. Precisely in the reigns of Domitian and Trajan we have reports of factional and more particularly class conflict in several cities of Asia, including Sardis, Smyrna, Aspendus, Prusa, Nicaea and Tarsus.[429] Bowersock comments that the Greek opposition (at least in the Augustan period) was not confined to the lower classes, but also that the latter were the core of discontent.[430] A revolt in Achaea is further reported under Antoninus Pius - the source this time is not only the Augustan History.[431] Rostovtzeff has noted the connection between the Cynic preachers of the period and the opposition to the Caesars,[432] which was such as to have appealed to the discontended proletariat. While similar opposition to Rome in Alexandria, certainly continuing into Trajan's reign if not beyond, and expressed in the notorious Acts of the Pagan Martyrs, elicits Cynic influence, but was also anti-Semitic - a case can be made for a link-up between the Cynic opposition, Judaism and the movement that culminated with the assassination of Domitian.[433]

Jewish literature has preserved one striking tradition datable to Hadrian's reign, which reflects Greek sympathy for the Jewish rebellion; a Midrash says,[434] in the name of R. Abba ben Kahana: "there have never lived philosophers like Bile'am son of Be'ior and Avnomos ha-Girdi." The reference is to the Cynic philosopher Oenomaos of Gadara, a contemporary of R. Meir (AD 140-165 , a pupil of R. 'Aqiva), with whom he was befriended. Oenomaos possessed a considerable knowledge of Judaism, and his outlook included several attitudes closely akin to those of its adherents. He published a sarcastic revelation of the deceptions practised by pagan oracles, and had delivered so savage an onslaught on idol-worship that its echoes are still to be heard in the writings of the Emperor Julian in the middle of the 4th century.[435] Midrash Genesis continues:[436] "All the gentiles of the world met at his [sc. Oenomaos'] house [and asked him, saying], Tell us, can we become one with this nation?

He said to them: Go and tarry by their synagogues and schools, and as long as you hear the voices of the children piping there, you cannot join them, for their Father pledged them, saying: The voice is the voice of Jacob; so long as the voice of Jacob is heard in the synagogues, the hands are not the hands of Esau, but if the voice of Jacob is not heard there, the hands are those of Esau, and you may join them."

It seems to me that this tradition reflects an authentic discussion among the Greeks of Judaea and its vicinity whether or not to join the Jewish rising against Hadrian. It is not unreasonable to associate this occasion with Gadara itself, as indeed the Jewish tradition suggests. The presence at Gadara of the legion XIV Gemina evidenced by an epitaph of one of its men,[437] if it belongs to the period 132-135, may not have been a coincidence. Whatever the case, the talmudic tradition does establish one important fact, namely, that there were Greek philosophers who understood the importance of Judaism as a factor in the struggle for human liberty against absolutism, and found common ground with Jewish thinking. These men were active in the same period among the Greek urban masses, hence it is not impossible that there were elements amongst the latter who gave moral or active support to the Jewish movement against Rome in Hadrian's time.[438]

BEN KOSBA AS MILITARY LEADER

It is not the purpose of the present paper to examine the religious and mystical aspects of the Jewish movement led by Simon ben Kosba. But it is possible that the conclusions reached in the preceding pages permit a certain evaluation of the Jewish leader as a military commander, and of the quality of his forces.

Firstly, their social composition. We have seen that the backbone of the Jewish movement and the original initiative in dissident action were derived first and foremost from the rural population. The participation of craftsmen is made probable by Dio's allusion to the deliberate production of defective weapons for the Roman army.[439] This belief is reinforced by the evidence of the coinage of the revolutionary government, which was of outstanding artistic quality.[440] Clearly other strata of the community were drawn into the revolt as it developed; R. 'Aqiva, though always in active sympathy with the underdog, was well-to-do in later life,[441] as was Simon ben Gamliel, who is known to have survived the siege of Bethar.[442] On the other hand we have an extremely interesting passage in Jer. Gittin [443] relating how the ba'alei batim (בעלי בתים) grabbed the Jewish lands confiscated and sold up by the Roman authorities after the revolt. The term ba'alei batim is the Hebrew equivalent of the οἰκοδεσπόται of the Gospels, and are always estate-owners with tenants and labourers. Some scholars take the Hebrew term to denote the small peasants of halakhic literature, but in this case it is evident that rich landowners, more especially non-Jews, are meant; their Greek identity is made clear by the opening of the passage.[444] This suggests that the wealthy elements of the Greek cities were more particularly hostile to the movement, as might be expected. Such elements may have included a Jewish group; we have the interesting example of Barsimso son of Callisthenes, who enlisted at Caesarea in the Cohors I Vindelicorum MCR in 132.[445] That he was a Jew rather than an Aramaic and Greek-speaking gentile, may be assumed from his first name, hardly one to be borne by a non-Jew in that mixed city. This does not mean, however, that there may not have been sympathizers with the Jewish movement in some Greek cities; we have noted the Jewish tradition relating to Oenomaos of Gadara.

It is also probable, however, that there was a further section of the Jewish community which, while sympathetic to the rising, preferred to adopt a non-commital attitude. This is evidenced by Justin, whose Dialogue with Tryphon[446] was presumably based on a measure of current reality when it described young Jewish refugees[447] in Ephesus who had escaped thither from the war. It is to be noted that Tryphon and his friends spoke Greek, and Tryphon himself, a man of good education,[448] accustomed to conversing with Greek gentiles, had studied Socratic philosophy in Argos.

The main cadres of the Jewish force may be thought to have acquired considerable experience in guerilla warfare in the hill country in the course of the years prior to 132. How far there was continuity of tradition from the activist groups of 66-73 is problematic; the Sicarian link with the inception of the war preserved by Jer. Ber., I, 5 and Mid. Lamentations Rabbah (I, 16) (above pp. 16, 17), suggests that such may have existed. How far the Diaspora revolt of 115-117 contributed experience or manpower cannot be determined; a Murabba'at document[449] records the presence of one Hillel of Cyrene among the Jewish combatants. There were Jews from Cyrene living at Jaffa in the years after the diaspora revolt, and it may be no coincidence that there is suspicion of disturbance in the harbour-town in the years 115-117. (Above, p. 18.) Generally the Jews of Judaea suffered from a break in the military tradition created by the Maccabees, since Herod's Jewish troops had mutinied in 4 BCE,[450] and the trained elements in 66 consisted chiefly of Babylonian and Idumaean Jews loyal to Agrippa II, concentrated in Bashan and Hauran,[451] and of the Jews of Idumaea itself.[452] The Jewish military elements stationed in the first two areas had been assimilated to the Roman army or transferred elsewhere some time after 108.[453] The Idumaeans of the south were annihilated in 66-70.

Three points may be made relating to Jewish fighting morale. 1) Any continuity of activist tradition from the years 66 or 115 would have meant a predominantly offensive attitude.[454] This would be manifested by much élan in sudden attack and a talent for guerilla operations, but less by a capacity for action in large formations against similar forces in the field. 2) Some groups, at least, of Ben Kosba's men were organized in brotherhoods, since they are referred to as ἀδελφοί [455], implying a common ideology. 3) The tradition of Midrash Lamentations Rabba[456] in which Ben Kosba is said to have tested the mettle of his volunteers by making them uproot a cedar at full gallop, if it contains any germ of historical value, points to a policy of strict selectivity in enrolment.[457] This deduction ties in logically with the record of fraternal organization which has reached us.

On the size of the Jewish forces there is no point in speculating. But one subject is relevant, to wit, the view expressed by some scholars that Ben Kosba enforced compulsory military service. Alon sees evidence for this in the tradition that the Christians were persecuted by the new régime. This tradition takes two forms: the first is that of Justin[458] who claims that they were persecuted for their faith, i.e. - by inference - that they refused to acknowledge Ben Kosba as the Messiah; the second, found in Eusebius,[459] in Jerome,[460] Syncellus[461] and in Michael Syriacus,[462] conveys that they were persecuted because they refused to join the Jewish forces. Michael the Syrian, admittedly the latest of these sources, writes explicitly that Ben Kosba forced "all mortals" to join the struggle against Rome. The second version may well be the correct one, since, as Alon points out,[463] R. 'Aqiva's claim that Ben Kosba was the King-Messiah[464] was not accepted by R. Yohanan ben Torta,[465] while the fact is thoroughly attested by his coins and by the Judaean Desert documents that he bore the official title, not of king or messiah, but of Nasi,[466] like the first Hasmoneans before him[467] and the Patriarchs after him.[468] Accordingly it was probably for their refusal to obey a decree of universal conscription that the Christians of Judaea were persecuted.[469]

It is not clear how far Simon Ben Kosba commanded Jewish military operations from the very beginning. Apart from the difficulty of determining a definite point in time at which Jewish resistance began, since there is evidence (above, pp. 17-22) of a prolonged state of ferment and guerrilla activity before 132 - Jewish tradition does contain a hint that Ben Kosba appeared as supreme commander only after open war had been declared. Midrash Lamentations Rabba and B. Gittin embody three distinct traditions, namely, 1) that concerning the operations of the brothers of Kefar Ḥarrubah who decide to proclaim Ben Kosba king;[470] 2) that which tells of Ben Kosba's selection of his fighting men and of his personal prowess, but ascribes to him the same slogan as that attributed by the first tradition to the brothers of Kefar Ḥarrubah;[471] 3) B. Gittin,[472] having described the Roman-Jewish clash at Tur Malka (Har ha-Melekh) (above, p. 15), relates the achievements of Bar Daroma, a native of that area, against Hadrian, putting into his mouth the slogan attributed by the former traditions to the men of Kefar Ḥarrubah and to Ben Kosba respectively. It is possible to follow Yeivin,[473] who sees in this slogan a battle-cry common to the entire Jewish movement, but it seems to me that the relevant conclusion to be drawn from these traditions is that a number of Jewish partisan groups were operating in various areas, and that their coalescence under one leader - Ben Kosba - took place when the phase of critical success was being approached in the years 131-2, doubtless under the impact of Hadrian's decision to build Aelia and of the reinforcement of the Roman garrison.[474] While the first midrashic tradition and B. Gittin credit other Jewish commanders with the slogan, in the second it has been absorbed by Ben Kosba - surely a likely and almost inevitable process characteristic of the mythopoeic activity flowing from the latter's increased prestige.

It is possible to point to several fairly well-attested items of information that suggest disunity among the Jewish resistance,[475] but one outstanding fact may be taken to indicate an almost monolithic unity at least in the first phase of the preparation and implementation of the rising. This is the successful concealment of those preparations, which has emerged from an examination of the sources in the present enquiry. (Above, p. 20). The first major success of the rising was the choice, for the purpose of preparing the attack, of a district removed from the densely populated areas and accessible only with the greatest difficulty to the police and the army. If the Roman intelligence was not hoodwinked, they remained ignorant of the true scope of the impending rising and were thus misled into a wrong appreciation of its true proportions.

The second achievement was the isolation and ultimate reduction of the castella held by the Roman auxiliary and other garrisons at various points. The major by-product of this achievement was to isolate the X Fretensis at Jerusalem and probably to cause the evacuation of the city by the legion.[476] Such an evacuation may well have been delayed by the fact that the decision had been taken to build Aelia on the site. The isolation of the castella was achieved by the exploitation of the country's topographical fragmentation, whose tactical implications have already been clarified (above, pp. 43 sq.). It could only be effected by a continuous activity which kept each of the garrisons in its own area and so prevented a Roman military concentration capable of conducting a general offensive sweep.

It is unlikely that such a plan occurred to a number of Jewish commanders individually, and if it did, coordination between them was needed if it was to succeed. The method argues an original mind, a directing hand, and a man who had studied the country and the Roman army, and drawn conclusions upon which a methodical plan could be based. This implies that Ben Kosba's influence had extended beyond his own district (perhaps that of Bethlehem, Hebron and the Wilderness of Judaea) before the rising.

The whole plan involved an offensive tactic. The question is, how far did the same original military mind come to grips with the second major problem, namely, the maintenance of the offensive after the hill-country had been successfully overrun, in order to win the lowlands? Ben Kosba doubtless knew something of the past, and he may have been more than aware of the failures of the Jewish offensives mounted in the war of 66-73. His problem was to develop the degree of tactical solidity, training and armament which would enable him to encounter the Roman forces on an equal footing in the plains. There was probably no solution. The chief offensive infantry weapons might be furnished; body armour, shields and helmets offered a more formidable problem; cavalry may well have been unattainable. In one branch, perhaps, the Jews could compete; they were competent javelin-throwers and almost certainly skilful slingers. It is controversial how far they used the bow. The question demands a more detailed enquiry, and it has been maintained that the laws of ritual slaughter restricted the use by Jews of the bow as a hunting weapon. Light cavalry armed with bows are nevertheless mentioned in the War Scroll,[477] and may have been alluded to once elsewhere in that work with reference to the skirmishers.[478] It may further be observed that the majority of the archer units of the Roman army came from the oriental provinces, and that some of them were recruited from the immediate vicinity of Judaea or from Judaea itself; they included the cohorts of Ituraei, Petraei and Ascalonitae.[479] Syria contributed no fewer than nine such units to the Roman army.[480] It has been stated[481] that the Ituraei were armed with the composite oriental bow which was so very superior in range and power to the small simple bow used in other Mediterranean countries;[482] but the bows with which two archers, one an Ituraean, are represented on German tombstones,[483] seem doubtfully to be of the composite type. On the other hand it is a fairly safe assumption that the Babylonian Jews who served under Zamaris' command in Agrippa II's kingdom in the 1st century AD, were armed with the composite weapon, a characteristically Parthian arm. Arrowheads have been found in three of the caves held by Ben Kosba's men,[484] hence it is not improbable that the bow formed part of the equipment of his forces. The weight of the arrowheads found in the Judaean caves, however, leaves little doubt that they belonged to a very small weapon, certainly not of the composite type.[485] Generally their skill in missiles endowed the Jews with a great tactical advantage; occupying commanding ground in the broken country they could pin down considerable bodies of the enemy and inflict numerous casualties upon them.[486]

The basic problem, however, of extending the offensive to the level country, remained unsolved. If the Jewish commander decided to meet the Romans only on ground of his own choosing, the decision meant a postponement of operations in the lowlands or a withdrawal therefrom. In that case, the only hope was attrition, that is, the exploitation of the hill-terrain to cause such difficulties and casualties to the enemy, even extending to the loss of large units, that their offensive came to a standstill. Probably the method succeeded, and led to the dissolution of XXII Deioteriana. It produced the inevitable Roman reaction - the concentration of Roman forces so massive, and so constituted from the point of view of tactical adaptability to the terrain, that they were able to carry out the slow, methodical and relentless isolation of topographically defended areas, till they were liquidated one after the other, and the Jewish initiative was lost in the process.[487] Even when forced onto the defensive, it seems, Ben Kosba did not make the mistake of which his Jewish forebears were guilty in the war of 66-73. He avoided a vast Jewish concentration in Jerusalem, and generally forebore to undertake the defence of urban settlements burdened by uncommitted elements and non-combatants. The fifty strongholds ultimately captured by Julius Severus were improbably urban sites, and not a single town is mentioned by any of the Jewish traditions connected with the war. It is indeed not improbable, although no more than a hypothesis, that one of the sources of Jewish disunity in the earlier phases of the struggle was the refusal of the Nasi to rehabilitate Jerusalem.

CONCLUSIONS

1. The majority of the folk-traditions preserved by talmudic literature concerning the outbreak and course of the Second Jewish Revolt of 132-135 point to an origin among the Jewish rural elements. These traditions are supported by the information transmitted by the same sources, whether halakhic or midrashic, on the agrarian situation in Judaea subsequent to the year 70. They describe great tenurial oppression caused by the alienation of the land to Roman landlords or their representatives, and to other gentile or pro-Roman elements. There is also evidence for the growth of imperial domain in the province, and some support for this is furnished by the documents of Ben Kosba's administration found in the caves of the Judaean desert.

2. The above evidence enables a conclusion concerning the principal social element which created the rising and constituted its backbone; this was, as in the first revolt, the peasantry. This circumstance would explain the tactical aptitudes and methods of the forces of Ben Kosba.

3. The question of the initial geographical extent of the rising is in a fluid state, but its initial focus and nerve-centre have become clear thanks to the discoveries in the Judaean desert.

4. A period of prior periodical disturbance in Judaea and of guerilla warfare is probable. Scholarly traditions suggest a number of local leaders increasingly influenced by an outstanding leader - Ben Kosba.

5. The problem of the capture of Jerusalem during the rising is still unsolved. One of the causes of Jewish failure in the first revolt was the vast concentration of Jewish forces and civilians in the city. In general the involvement of the Jewish resistance with urban centres containing non-combatants and neutral or hostile elements was a potent cause of failure in the same war. Ben Kosba may have recognized this and have avoided reoccupying the capital.

6. The Jewish commander devised a tactic and a strategy adapted to the Roman military dispositions, to the aptitudes of his recruits and to the country's terrain. It was successful to the point that it brought the Roman forces in the province, even in their initially reinforced state, to a standstill. But it could not solve the problem of the offensive in level country against overwhelming forces augmented from outside.

7. In spite of valuable experience in Dacia and Britain, the rising found the Roman forces of the eastern Empire weak in two respects: 1) in intelligence and reconnaissance; 2) in fighting in hilly country, more especially in wooded and rocky terrains. These needs probably gave an added impulse to the subsequent development of the _numeri_, whose aptitudes involved them in both activities.

8. A comparison with the Roman military occupation of Wales, as revealed by recent investigations, forcibly suggests that the ultimate Roman aim was the extermination of the Jewish population of Judaea.

9. Dio's allusion to the participation of non-Jews in the rising has been neglected and requires further study. Some evidence suggests that attention should be devoted to the situation in Arabia and to the attitude of certain elements in the Greek cities of the eastern Empire.

10. A study of the intellectual and religious forces behind the revolt is not the aim of the present essay. It should nevertheless be noted that there exists the tradition of a lineal connection between the movement and the Sicarian group (Menahem), and of a messianic aspiration; also of a militant scholarly group dissenting from the rabbinical majority. Devir has pointed to resemblances between the leadership of the revolutionary constitution as interpretable from the coins, and the constitution adumbrated in the Qumran records, also to resemblances between the ideas of the militant group and those expressed in the literature of the Qumran sect.

Tel Aviv University
The Dept. of Jewish History.

APPENDIX

ROMAN AUXILIARY UNITS WHICH SERVED, OR PROBABLY SERVED,
IN HADRIAN'S JEWISH WAR

I. COHORTS

1. I. Breucorum cR. In Raetia A.D. 121-125 (AE 61, no. 173). At Pfünz under Antoninus Pius the cohort bears the titles Valeria victrix bis torquata ob v(irtutem) appella(ta), which can only be ascribed to Hadrian's Jewish War. (Radnóti, Germania, 39, 1961, pp. 114 sqq.).

2. III Bracaraugustanorum. The cohort was in Raetia in 107 and 147 (CIL. XVI, p. 180), in Syria-Palaestina in 139 (A.E. 97, no. 106).

3. IIII Bracaraugustanorum. CIL. VIII 7079 (Cirta) records C. Aufidius Maximus as prefect of this cohort "in Iudaea". This is confirmed by the diploma CIL. XVI, no. 87, listing units in Syria-Palaestina in 139.

4. IIII Callaecorum. CIL. XVI, no. 103, a diploma dated 134-154, lists this unit; as it is fragmentary, it is uncertain whether the units recorded belong to Syria or to Syria-Palaestina. Nesselhauf (ad. loc.) thinks rather Syria, but it mentions the Ala VII Phrygum, known independently to have been in Syria-Palaestina in 139.

5. II Cantabrorum. In Judaea in A.D. 86 according to Dip. CIL. XVI, no. 33 of that year.

6. I Damascenorum. In Egypt in 135 on the evidence of the papyri BGU 73, and 135, also of CIL. V, 5126; in Syria-Palaestina by 139 according to CIL. XVI, 87. Hence it is uncertain whether the cohort arrived in Judaea in time to be in action against Ben Kosba's men, but it might have taken part in "mopping up" operations.

7. I Flavia cR E. In Moesia in 80 (AE. 48, no. 56), it had moved to Syria by 88 (CIL. XVI, no. 35) and in 139 is found in Syria-Palaestina (CIL. XVI, no. 87).

8. I Ulpia Galatarum. In Syria-Palaestina in 139. (CIL. XVI, no. 87).

9. II Ulpia Galatarum. Likewise.

10. IIII Gallorum. This cohort is known to have been in Raetia and Moesia in the years 105 (CIL. XVI, no. 50), 107 (CIL. XVI, no. 55), 154/61 (AE. 22, no. 50), 156/7 (CIL. XVI, no. 183), 150/70 (CIL. XVI, no. 106), in Syria or Syria-Palaestina 134/54 (CIL. XVI, no. 103) and in Syria 156/7 (CIL. XVI, 106). If the same unit was in-

volved throughout, it must have been transferred to Syria before 154 and returned to Raetia before 156, and once again gone to Syria in the latter year. But if two units are concerned, one could have reached Syria-Palaestina any time in 134 or later down to 154. Cf. the alleged disturbances in Judaea under Pius, (here p.56 and n.417).

11. VII Gallorum is recorded in Syria or Syria-Palaestina in 134/154 (CIL. XVI, no. 103). Which province was then its station, and whether it arrived under Hadrian, depends on the same considerations as those affecting nos. 4 and 10 above.

12. V Gemina cR. (= V Gemella cR). In Syria-Palaestina in 139 (CIL. XVI, no. 87). A tribune of this cohort is recorded as its commander after having served as tribune in legion X Fretensis (AE. 35, no. 167).

13. IIII Lingonum E. In Britain in 103 (CIL. XVI, no. 48). For its transfer to the Jewish War under Hadrian, see above, pp. 48-49. (CIL. VI, 1523). The cohort was again in Britain in 146 according to Dip. LVII (CIL. XVI, no. 93).

14. I Lucensium E. In Syria A.D. 91 (AE. 61, no. 319). In Syria or Syria-Palaestina in 134/154 (CIL. XVI, no. 103).

15. I Montanorum. In Dacia in 110 (AE. 44, no. 58). 139 in Syria-Palaestina (CIL. XVI, no. 87), if this is the same unit, for in November of the same year it is recorded in Pannonia Inferior (CIL. XVI, no. 175) - cf. Nesselhauf in CIL. XVI, ad no. 31. There is a further record in Pannonia (AE. 44, no. 102) for the year 148.

15. IV Petraeorum S. (Van de Weerd, Lambrechts, Laureae Aquincenses, I, p. 231). Syria-Palaestina in 139 (CIL. XVI, no. 87).

16. VI (Ulpia.) Petraeorum S. (Van de Weerd, Lambrechts, loc. cit., p. 232). Syria-Palaestina in 139 (CIL. XVI, no. 87).

17. I. Sebastenorum M cR. In Syria in 91 (AE. 61, no. 319); in Syria-Palaestina in 139 (CIL. XVI, no. 87). QDAP XII, 1946, p. 96 = AE. 48, no. 151, records a soldier of a coh. cR.m.S (ebast) at Samaria. The cohort was in Syria in 157.

18. V Augusta cR Sebastena. AE. 48, no. 150 = QDAP XII, 1946, pp. 94-95 records a tesserarius of Coh.V (Augustae?) cR (Sebastenae?) at Samaria.

19. I Claudia Sygambrorum (veterana) E. Transferred from Moesia after 134 (CIL. XVI, no. 106, adnot. 1). It was in Syria in 157 (CIL. XVI, no. 106).

20. I Thebaeorum. In Egypt in 93 (CIL. XVI, no. 29). In Judaea in 105 (AE. 68, no. 513 - extranslatarum in Iudaeam - and again in Egypt in 156 (CIL. XVI, no. 184).

21. I Thracum = Coh.I Augusta Thracum M. In Syria in A.D. 91 just after it had been raised to a cohors miliaria (AE. 61, no. 319). In Judaea in 124, at least part at 'Ein Geddi (Yadin, Polotzky, BIES

XXVI, 1962, p. 239). This appears to be the Coh. I Thracum m. Syriaca of CIL. XVI, no. 87, in Syria-Palaestina in 139.

22. I Thracum E. In Judaea in 89 (CIL. XVI, no. 33). Mann, IEJ XIX, 1969, p. 213, equates this unit with Coh. I Augusta Thracum which left an epitaph at Mampsis (Kurnub) in the early 2nd century.

23. III Augusta Thracum cR E. In Raetia in 107 (CIL. XVI, no. 55). AE. 11, no. 161 records a prefect of the unit who commanded Trajan's Parthian War, i.e. probably under Hadrian. Radnoti, Germania, 39, 1961, p. 114, notes that the unit, when stationed at Gnotzheim in A.D. 144, bore the title bis torquata, evidently a distinction won in Judaea under Hadrian.

24. I. Vindelicorum. M cR Pia Fidelis. In Moesia Superior in 110 (CIL. XVI, no. 163). It was at Caesarea Maritima in Judaea in 132 (CIL. XVI, no. 107). By A.D. 144 it had reached Dacia Superior (CIL. XVI, no. 90).

II. ALAE

25. I Flavia Gemina. In Germania Superior in 116 (CIL. XVI, nos. 62, 63). It was no longer in the province in 134 (CIL. XVI, no. 80). Its transfer to Judaea under Hadrian is therefore possible; cf. Radnoti, Germania, loc. cit.

26. Flavia Gaetulorum = ? Ala I Flavia Gaetulorum. In Pannonia Inferior in 114 (CIL. XVI, 58, 61); at Beyrut under Hadrian (AE. 12, no. 179). CIL. VI, 3505 records S. Attilius Senecio, praefectus alae Flaviae Gaetulorum trib. leg.X Gem., missus a divo Hadriano in expeditionem Iudaicam ad vexxillationes deducendas. Presumably Attilius was sent with the vexillation as tribune of X Gemina, but the ala Flavia Gaetulorum may well have accompanied the legion; cf. the plural vexillationes; also the Ala Gaetulorum recorded in Arabia in the 2nd or 3rd century by SEG. XXIV, 1064 (Tomi) - ἔπαρχος ἱπ(π)έων εἴλης Γαιτούλων τῶν ἐν Ἀραβίᾳ . But the Cohort was again in Pannonia Inferior in 151/160 (CIL. XVI, no. 112).

27. Gallorum et Thracum. In Syria, in 91 (AE. 61, no. 319). In Syria-Palaestina in 139 (CIL. XVI, no. 87). The Ala Gallorum et Thracum Classiana cR found in Wales 98-105 (Nash-Williams, Jarrett, The Roman Frontier in Wales, 1969, p. 16), and in 122 (AE. 30, no. 37) has been regarded as the same unit (E.Birley, JRS., XXII, 1932, p. 59), but this seems to me doubtful.

28. Gallorum et Thraecum Antiana. In Syria-Palaestina in 139 (CIL. XVI, no. 87) where it is called the Ala Antiana Gallorum.

29. VII Phrygum. Its presence in Syria under Trajan and Hadrian is evident from AE. 25, 44 (Albertini, Inscrs. d'Algérie, p. xiv = CIL. VIII, 9365), which records an officer twice prefect of this

ala under the former emperor, then tribune in legions XII Fulminata and XII Scythica, then commanding officer of Coh.I Flavia cR E, all known to have been contemporarily in Syria or Syria-Palaestina. (Cf. AE., 38, no. 169, 171; CIL II, 4251. The cohort is found in Syria-Palaestina in 139 (CIL. XVI, no. 87).

30. I Scubulorum S (Van de Weerd, Lambrechts, loc. cit., p. 230). The ala is evidenced in Germania Superior for the years 74, 82, 90 and 116 (CIL. XVI, nos. 20, 28, 36, 62, 63); it is absent in 134 (ibid. no. 80); in this last diploma no alae are listed, hence this cavalry unit and the following, the only ones stationed in the province according to the preceding known diploma, had in all probability been sent to the Jewish war (A. Radnóti, Germania, 39, p. 115, n. 118).

31. I Picentiana. In Germania Superior in 74, 82, 90 and 116 (CIL. XVI, nos. 20, 28, 36, 62, 64); it is absent in the year 134. See Ala I Scubulorum above, and Radnóti, loc. cit.

32. I Thracum Mauretana. In Judaea in 86 (CIL. XVI, no. 33). In Egypt in 142 or before (M.G. Jarrett, IEJ XIX, 1969, p. 217).

FOOTNOTES

1. E. Schürer, Geschichte des Jüdischen Volkes in Zeitalter Jesu Christi, I, 1901, pp. 670-704.

2. G. Vermes, F. Millar, The History of the Jewish People in the Age of Jesus Christ, I, 1973, pp. 534 sqq. (Para. 21, III).

3. Jewish Quarterly Review, XVI, 1904, pp. 143 sqq.

4. I, 1954; II, 1955, pp. 1-47.

5. For an extensive interim report, Bull. of the Israel Exploration Society, XXVI, 1962, passim (Heb.).

6. Bar Kokhba, the Man and the Messiah, 1964 (Heb.).

7. Y. Meshorer, Jewish Coins in the Second Temple Period, 1967; Mildenberg, Schweizerische Numismatische Rundschau, 34, 1948, pp. 9, 19-27; L. Kadman, The Coins of Aelia Capitolina, 1956; A. Kindler, The Dating and Meaning of Ancient Jewish Coins, (Numismatic Studies and Researches, II), 1958, pp. 62 sqq.; B. Kanael, Altjüdische Münzen, Jahrbuch für Numismatik und Geldgeschichte, 1967, para. 17; M. Philonenko, CRAI 1974, pp. 183-189, with further bibliography.

8. Judaea, Samaria and the Golan; the Archaeological Survey, 1967-68, ed. M. Kokhbi, 1972: The Society for the Archaeological Survey of Israel. (Heb.).

9. Applebaum in Scripta Classica Israelica, I, 1974, pp. 116 sqq.; Domitian's Assassination: the Jewish Aspect.

10. B. AZ 10b; see Alon, op. cit., (n. 4), I, p. 74.

11. Hegesippus ap. Eusebius, HE III, 19, 20.

12. Ibid., III, 32, 3, 4.

13. Arrian, Diss. IV, 7, 6.

14. Dio, LXVII, 12, 1; 14, 2; Fronto, ad Marcum, 22, 23.

15. Y. Yadin, Finds from the Bar Kokhba Period in the Cave of the Letters (Judaean Desert Studies, I), 1963, pp. 123-124, and fig. 45.

16. M. Mattingley, Coins of the Roman Empire in the British Museum, III, 1966, p. 15, no. 88.

16a. Yet these abuses may have continued on a wider scale and at the expense of non-Jews in relation to other taxation under Trajan; cf. Aurelius Victor, Epit. de Caesaribus, 42, 21.

17. Hist., V, 1-10.

18. See Y. Levi, Worlds Meet (Heb.), 1960, pp. 115-196: Tacitus on Jewish History and Character.

19. P. Romanelli, CAH XI, 1930, pp. 248 sqq.; Schürer, GJV, Vermes, Millar, I, pp. 529 sqq.; Romanelli, Cirenaica romana, 1943, pp. 119 sqq.; A. Tcherikover, The Jews of Egypt in the Light of Papyri, 1943, Ch. vi, pp. 160 sqq. (Heb.-Eng. summary); CPJ II, 1960, pp. 225 sqq.; G. Alon, Hist. of the Jews of Eretz Yisrael, I, 1954, pp. 202 sqq. (Heb.); A. Fuks, JRS LI, 1961, pp. 98 sqq.; S. Applebaum, Jews and Greeks in Ancient Cyrene, 1969, pp. 224 sqq. (Heb.-Eng. résumé).

20. Eg. I Macc. v; II Macc. xii, 3; 9; 26; I Macc. x, 71; xi, 60-62; xiii, 11 etc.; Jos., BJ II, 457-98.

21. For the use of the word in inscriptions at Cyrene, cf. Africa Italiana, I, 1927, p. 321; ibid., p.318; JRS XL 1950, p. 89, D4; SEG IX, 168 etc. For the legal denotation of the term, Cic. VIII Phil., 2; CIL II, 5439; lines 26 sqq.; Liv. XXXIV, 56; Daremberg-Saglio, Dict. des ants. gr. et rom., V, p. 532, sv. tumultus.

22. Cf. Petronius' estimate in the reign of Gaius (Philo, Leg. ad Gaium, 31, para. 216 (Smallwood), of the danger to be anticipated from a combination of the Jews of the Empire and those of Parthia; also the midrash on B. AZ 10b and Ta'anit 3b: "Just as the world cannot exist without the winds, so it cannot exist without Israel... They would call you (the Empire) a kingdom that had been maimed." - i.e. the Dispersion is conceived as a safeguard of Jewish survival.

23. Cf. A. von Domaszewski, Gesch. der römischen Kaiser, 1909, II, pp. 202-3.

24. Cf. Syme, Tacitus, I, 1958, pp. 241, 244-5; II, p. 488.

25. Cf. CAH, XI, pp. 320, 587, sqq.

26. For the classification of the majority of the Jews with those liable to the laographia i.e. the native Egyptians, CPJ I, 1957, p. 60. Dr. A. Kasher has however shown, in his D. Phil. thesis, that there were Jewish inhabitants of the metropoleis in the Egyptian chora who, as people of Greek culture, paid the reduced rate of the laographia. This would mean, a fortiori, that there were hellenized Jews in Alexandria who benefited from the same rebate.

27. BJ II, 457-89.

28. Vespasian was already granting Roman citizenship to inhabitants of Gerasa - cf. R. O. Fink, JRS XXIII, 1933, p. 121 for the settlement here of auxiliary veterans with civitas.

29. The successors of Herod's Zamarid force, planted to guard the Jewish traffic from Mesopotamia and Babylonia to Judaea, were merged in the army of Agrippa II and some time in Trajan's reign (c. A.D. 108 - cf. Syria, XLII, 1965, pp. 31-34) combined with some other unit entitled "Augusta" and moved to Cappadocia, where they are found under Arrian's command in 135 (Ectaxis, I, 9) as the Ala Augusta Gemina Colonorum (οἱ ἀπὸ τῆς εἴλης ᾗ ὄνομα Κολωνοί ; CIL VIII, 8934; Ritterling, Wiener Studien, XXIV, 1902, pp. 361-2).

30. SHA Had., XX, 10: sacra Romana diligentissime curavit, peregrina contempsit.

31. Chron. Pascale, Dindorff, I, 474 (PG XLII, 614, para. 254).

32. BJ III, 289; IV, 450.

33. Syme, Tacitus, I, p. 31; his governorship: ILS 8970; cf. CRAI 1951, p. 255.

34. Dio (Ep.), LXIX, 1, 2.

35. ILS 9491.

36. SEG XX, 157 = AJA LXV, 1961, pp. 124-5.

37. Sifra Emor, 9, 5; Jer. Ta'an., II (13), 66a; Mid. Gen. Rab. 64, 10 etc.; Applebaum, JJS II, 1950, pp. 29 sqq.; Smallwood, Historia XI, 1962, p. 505.

38. Eus., Chron. (Helm), p. 197; ibid., ad ann. 2133 (PG XIX, 555).

39. SEG IX, 54; PBSR XXVI, 1958, p. 164; Robert, R ét G., LXXIII, 1960, pp. 207-208; ASAA XXXIX-LX, 1963, no. 68, p. 257; JRS XL 1950, pp. 77 sqq. (The supervision of the gymnasia of Cyrene and the incorporation of communities into the Panhellenion.)

40. SEG XX, 157 = AJA LXV, 1961, pp. 124-5.

41. Mid. Gen. Rab. 64, 10, Epiphanius, De mens. et pond. PG XLIII, 260-1, cap. 14; Alexander Monach., de inventione sanctae crucis, PG LXXXVII, iii, 4044-5; Ep. Barnabas, XVI, 1, 4 - Kirsopp Lake, pp. 126, 411; L. Finkelstein, Akiba, 1936, ed. 1962, pp. 313 sqq.

42. Op. cit., I, pp. 272-289.

43. See W. Weber in CAH, XI, 1954, ch. viii, especially pp. 319 sqq.

43a. Eus. Hieron., (Helm), Chron. ad ann. 125, p. 199; Dio LXIX, 11, 1; SHA Had., XIII, 1.

44. Paus., Att., I, 18, 6; Dio LXIX, 16, 1, 2; SHA Had., XIII, 6. For the date, Weber, Untersuchungen zur Gesch. des Kaisers Hadrianus, 1907, p. 268.

45. G. Richter, AJA XXXII, 1928, p. 6.

46. Cf. Paus., Elis, I, 12, 4: Ἐν δὲ τῇ Ὀλυμπίᾳ παραπέτασμα ἐρῦν κεκοσμένην ὑφάσμασιν Ἀσσυρίοις καὶ βαφῇ πορφύριας τῆς Φοινίκων ἀνέθηκεν Ἀντίοχος .....
For a discussion of the question whether the curtain described by Pausanias was the veil of the Temple, Pelletier, Syria, XXXII, 1955, pp. 288 sqq., who comes to a negative conclusion. The idea was originally suggested by Clermont Ganneau in Jour. asiatique, 1878, pp. 56 sqq.

47. SHA Had., XIII, 7.

48. Dio LXIX, 16, 1: τὸ τε Ὀλύμπειον τὸ ἐν ταῖς Ἀθήναις ἐν ᾧ καὶ αὐτὸς ἵδρυται.

49. SHA loc. cit.; et aram sibi.

50. CIA III, 471-525; Paus., Att. I, 18, 6.

51. See generally Weber, Untersuch. (n. 44), pp. 209 sqq. At Cyrene the Temple of Apollo, slowly restored in the course of the 2nd century after it had been wrecked by the tumultus Iudaicus of 115-117, contained Hadrian's image beside that of Apollo, placed, it would seem, in the first period of rehabilitation (Smith, Porcher, A History of the Discoveries at Cyrene, 1864, no. 63, p. 42).

52. On the Panhellenion, M. Tod, JHS LXII, 1922, pp. 173 sqq.

53. SHA Had., XIV, 1. See below, p. 57.

54. Cat. of Rom. Coins of the British Museum: Coins of the Rom. Emp., III, 1936, p. 512, no. 1757, Pl. 95, 3.

55. Ibid., pp. clxxix, clxxx; see also J. Toynbee, The Hadrianic School, 1934, pp. 117 sqq.; Mattingley, Sydenham, Rom. Imperial Coinage, II, 1926, p. 332. Izaak doubts the divine character of Professor Toynbee's "Greek standing goddess". Perhaps an allegorical figure would be a more rational description.

56. Had., XIV, 8, 11; XV, 1-13: in omnibus artibus peritissimus, tamen professores omnium artium semper ut doctior risit contempsit obtrivit.

57. Dio LXIX, 3, 3-6: ὁ δὲ δὴ φθόνος αὐτοῦ δεινότατος ἐς πάντας τοὺς τινι προέχοντας ὢν............βουλόμενος γὰρ πάντων ἐν πᾶσι περιεῖναι ἐμίσει τοὺς ἔν τινι ὑπεραίροντας.

57a. Cf. Aur. Victor, Epit. de Caesaribus, 14, 6-8: ingenium invidum -- dissimulans ardorem gloriae, qua flagrabat.

58. See p. 23. For Roman military epitaphs, not, unfortunately, closely datable, see Schwabe, ap. Yeivin, Hirschberg, Eretz Kinnarot, 1951 (Heb.), pp. 59 sqq.; QDAP XII, 1946, p. 91.

59. Epiph., Haer., 30, 12 (PG, XLI, 246).

60. Jer. AZ IV, 4, 43.

61. SHA Had. XIV, 4; Appian, B. Civ. II, 86; in II, 90 Appian seems to have confused this tomb with the Nemeseion just outside Alexandria.

62. Cf. Appian, B. Civ. II, 90, but better II, 86, where the desecration of the tomb's statues is recorded - a feature especially characteristic of the tumultus Iudaicus (see Bull. soc. roy. d'arch. d'Alex., XXXIX, 1951, p. 91, no. 5; PBSR XXVI, 1958, pp. 31-3; SEG IX, 136; JEA XVII, 1931, pp. 81 sqq.; and generally Applebaum, JGAC, pp. 231-247).

63. Ant. XIV, pp. 71-2.

64. For all this, Henderson, The Life and Principate of the Emperor Hadrian, 1923, pp. 131 sqq. Interesting is CIL VI, 8991 (ILS 7741), the epitaph of a seventeen year-old youth of Semitic extraction, consummatus litteris, who died at the praetorium of Hadrian in Rome while studying

there. Could he have been a predecessor of Antinous, and could his fate have contributed in some way to Hadrian's peculiar attitude to Judaism? The implications are unpleasant, but all remains conjecture.

65. M. Aurelius' silence, Henderson, op.cit., p. 133; Julian's satire, Autok., 311D; contemporary Christian criticism, Justin, I Apol., 29 (PG VI, 373).

66. Orac. Sib. (Geffken), III, 764; V, 166, 387. Cf. op.cit., VIII, 57: (Hadrian) παῖδα θεὸν δείκνυσει, ἅπαντα σεβάσματα λύσει Surely this rhyme was extraneous to the Oracula and a popular folk-catch among contemporary Jewry. Mme. Huteau-Dubois (loc.cit., pp. 173-174) has grasped the importance of the Hadrian-Antinous relationship as a factor contributing to the Jewish rising, but appears to see the main provocation in Antinous' deification, rather than in Hadrian's practice of homosexuality. The sources suggest that both elements should be accorded equal weight.

67. BJ VII, 217; Dio LXVI, 7, 2; Tcherikover, Fuks, CPJ I, pp. 80-1.

68. SHA Had., XIV, 2.

69. Hist. of the Jews of Eretz Yisrael, II, p. 12.

69a. For this reason I do not find much relevance in the additional passages cited by Smallwood (e.g. M. Avot, III, 12) with regard to epispasma and recircumcision (Latomus, XX, 1961, pp. 93-6). Even Hadrian's prohibition would not have affected those already circumcised.

70. B. BB. 60b.

71. Alon, op.cit., I, p. 262; II, p. 12.

72. Ki tisa, Shabbata, par. 1, p. 343 (Horowitz).

73. Para. 141.

74. Vermes, Millar, Hist. Jew. People, I, p. 536, and n. 96. See now F. Grelle, L'autonomia cittadina fra Traiano e Adriano, 1972, pp. 226-31, cited by Bowersock, JRS 75, p. 185, that Xiph. epit. Dio is the only source for Hadrian's temple. The Ep. Barnabas seems to be a clear allusion, however.

75. Latomus, XVIII, 1959, pp. 336-7.

76. Dig. Iust. Aug., II (Mommsen), pp. 820-1, XLVIII, 11,1.

77. LXIX, 12. 1-2.

78. HE IV, 6, 4.

79. Y. Meshorer, Jewish Coins of the Second Temple Period, 1966, pp. 60-61.

80. The Hebron Mountains: Collected Sources and Articles, Dept. of Local Studies of the Qibbutz Movement, 1970, pp. 67-8 (Heb.).

81. BJ VII, 100-111; Ant. XII, 123-4.

82. Applebaum ap. Safrai, Stern (ed.), Compendium Rerum Iudaicarum, I, The Jewish People in the First Century, 1974, p. 460.

83. Mid. Deut. Rab., II, 15.

84. Jer. Shev. IV, 2, 35.

85. Ulp. Dig., XLVIII, 8. 4. 2; Modestinus, Dig. XLVIII, 8. 11.

85a. Jews' College Publication no. 4: The Economic Condition of Judaea after the Destruction of the Second Temple, 1912.

86. Ibid., pp. 29 sqq.; 40-41.

87. It is nevertheless not always clear in the cases cited by Buechler whether the lands concerned were owned or leased. For proprietorship, however, see pp. 37-39; transfer, p. 39 (M. BM, V, 3 etc.), and especially Tos. Gitt. I, 4; B. Gitt. 11a - a land-registration office of the Roman administration in the time of R. 'Aqiva (ibid., p. 41, n. 1). For further evidence, Safrai, Tarbiz, XXXV, 1966, pp. 307-310.

88. BJ IV, 444.

89. BJ VII, 216-7.

90. GJV I, p. 640, n.141; cf. Strabo, IV, 13, 188, on the lakes of Tolosa:
οἱ γὰρ Ῥωμαῖοι κρατήσαντες τῶν τόπων ἀπέδοντο
τὰς λίμνας δημοσίᾳ, καὶ τῶν ὠνησαμένων πολλοὶ
μύλους ηὗρον σφυρηλάτους ἀργυροῦς.
ὠνησαμένων according to Liddel and Scott, sv. ὠνέομαι (2), means "bid for, purchase the farming of public taxes and properties", e.g. ὠνέεσθαι μέταλλα Demosthenes, 19, 293.

91. There is some reason to think that Lydda was centred on royal domain land in the time of Hyrcanus II - cf. Ant. XIV, 208. Presumably this passed to Herod and ultimately to Augustus in AD 6. It might have returned to the Herods under Agrippa I or II, as the district was part of the King's Mountain (Har ha-Melekh), of which see below. If so, the Jewish estates round Lydda would have been granted by Vespasian out of the praedium Caesaris, much as lands were granted by him to Josephus in the plainland and in Judaea itself (Jos., Vita, 422, 425); but it might equally have been the gift of Agrippa II - a very attractive conjecture.

92. Dr. M. Gil in the Rev. internationale des droits de l'antiquité, XVII, 1970, pp. 40 sqq., argues that the term matziq derives from the Greek μεσίτης, an intermediary holding the deposits and mortgages of parties to a law-suit; later (in the 2nd century AD) as the Roman sequester, he could initiate an action to transfer the mortgaged property. The anas Gil connects (on the evidence of B. Sanh. 26a) with the word annona, i.e. he is an official who confiscates land forfeit for non-payment of that tax. It is difficult for philological reasons to accept the derivation of matziq from μεσίτης as suggested by Gil; nor is the connection with annona satisfactory, as will be seen from M. Kil. VII, 6. The mortgage procedure would hardly be relevant or necessary in conditions of rebellion or warfare, even in an established province.

92a. A reference in Mid. Siphri ad Deut. (Friedmann) p. 354, to matziqim at Tzoar, at the south end of the Dead Sea, outside Judaea till the establishment of Provincia Arabia in AD 106, furnishes a terminus post quem for the present text, but as the reference appears separately and after the list of districts affected by the matziqim, it is probably a later interpolation, and would push the text itself back into the 1st century of the current era.

93. These passages are discussed by S. Klein, Palästinensische Studien, I (Neue Beitrage zur Gesch. und Geographie Galiläas), 1923, pp. 28 sqq., but not from a Roman juridical point of view.

94. Sifre de-Bei-Rav, Friedmann, para. 149, p. 357; Mid. Tannaim, Hoffmann, pp. 223 sqq.

95. Friedmann, para. 317 on Deut. 31:13.

96. Hoffmann, p. 193.

97. These words, absent from Mid. Siph. ad Deut., are found in Mid. Tannaim, Hoffmann, p. 193.

97a. Mid. Sif. ad Deut. (Friedmann), p. 357, para. 149.

98. Tos. Betzah, II, 6.

99. The payment of agricultural produce to centurions is mentioned several times elsewhere in talmudic literature (e.g. Tos. Dem. VI, 3, 4); one case certainly refers to the payment of corn into a state granary; the other probably concerns discharge of the annona. The present instance sounds like the payment of produce to the army on prata legionis, and reminds us of the procedures on territorium legionis in the 3rd century. Cf. e.g. CIL V, 808; A. Móczy, Acta Ant. Hungarica, III, 1953, pp. 179 sqq.

100. Jer. Sota, III, 4, 19a; Mekhilta, 12, 48, p. 18a. Taking one kor as the seed to be sown on 23 dunams (2.3 hectares) (Y. Felicks, The Agric. of the Mishnah and the Talmud, 1963, p. 160), this would imply, on a seven-to-one yield, with fallow, an area of about 197 hectares or 493 acres approximately.

101. Rostovtzeff, SEHRE II, p. 562, n. 17; pp. 669 sqq., n. 45.

102. M. Kil. VII, 6.

103. M. Dem. VI, 2; Tos. Dem. VI, 3, 4; Jer. Dem. VI, 1, 25a.

104. E.g. M. Gitt. V, 6; Jer. Gitt. V, 6, 47a. For a detailed discussion of the problems involved, S. Safrai, Zion, XVII, 1952, pp. 56 sqq.

105. Some of the payments were to the annona militaris; see above n. 99.

106. Hist. of the Jews, I, p. 37.

107. Mid. Tannaim, Hoffmann, p. 198, para. 317.

109. IX, 2.

110. IX, 2, 38.

111. E.g. Tos. Ma'as. Sheni, I, 6.

112. I, 11.

113. 57a.

114. B.-Tz. Luria, King Yannai, 1961, pp. 28 sqq. (Heb.).

115. Tos. Shev., VII, 14.

116. 57a.

117. JQR XVI, 1904, p. 175.

118. Cf. The villages of Yannai restored to Hyrcanus II by senatorial decree at the instance of Julius Caesar (Ant. XIV, 207).

119. Jer. Ta'an. IV, 69a: B. Yoma 35b.

120. B. Yoma 9a.

121. Kleine Schriften, II, 1953, p. 386, n. 3.

122. Georgius Cedrenus, PG CXXI, p. 369, 330C. This is a late source, but as Narbattene was outside Antipas' tetrarchy, the report is likely to be correct. It is worth noting that excavations by the writer of a village-site at Tell Ibrekhtas not far south of Hadera (Israel grid 139.248) revealed a 2nd-century BC settlement which had been evacuated in the late 1st century BC and resettled almost immediately by cultivators of Semitic tradition, apparently non-Jews. This process seems best explicable by the assumption that the original settlers were removed in connection with the building of Caesarea and the formation of the new city's territory.

123. B. Yoma 35b.

123a. Cf. Mid. Lam. II, 4-5 (19, 20).

124. Ant. XIV, 208.

125. BJ VII, 217.

126. Despite the hyperbole of B. Yoma, R. Ele'azar ben Harsum's holdings were very large; of him is related the incident, which has every semblance of circumstantiality, of his seizure by his own tenants, who did not recognize him, to perform an angaria. (B. Yoma 35b).

127. P. Benoit, J. T. Milik, R. de Vaux, DJD II, Les grottes de Murabba'at, 1961, pp. 122 sq. no. 24A-F.

128. Yadin, IEJ XII, 1962, pp. 249 sqq., no. 42.

129. IEJ XI, loc. cit., no. 43.

130. Ibid., no. 44.

131. IEJ XII, no. 45.

132. Ibid., no. 46.

133. That this was regarded as the legal property of the Jewish commonwealth seems to be confirmed by the letter of Ben Kosba from the Nahal Hever cave (BIES XXV, 1961, no. 12, pp. 59-60), which rebukes Masbala and Yohanan bar Ba'in, "people of 'Ein Geddi", because they are "sitting and eating and drinking the property of the house of Israel nor caring for your brethren." Probably 'Ein Geddi had been royal property under Herod, and had passed to the Roman fiscus after the War of the Destruction (cf. Ant. IX, 7).

134. Murabba'at, pp. 134, 137, 144.

135. Ibid., nos. 24B, 8; C7-8; E6-7.

136. See Murabba'at and the Naḥal Ḥever documents passim.

137. CIL VIII, 26416, para. iii, line 6; Hyginus (Lachmann), p. 116.

138. IEJ XI, 1961, pp. 48-9.

139. Tos. Men. IX, 13; Tos. Dem. I, 11; B. Ber. 44a; Tos. Shev. VII, 12.

140. Cf. Jones, The Later Roman Empire, II, 1964, pp. 737-740, for the difficulties encountered in filling up the curial ranks of the cities in the later Empire. Cf. Jer. Mo'ed Qat. II, 3, 81a, (R. Yoḥanan, 3rd century): If you are proposed for the Boulé, let the Jordan be your frontier.

141. The subject is complex and should not be oversimplified. A high percentage of the Jewish town population cultivated lands (cf. Kreissig, Acta Ant. Hung. XVII, 1969, pp. 233 sqq.), but far the majority of the Jewish population down to the Second Revolt lived on the countryside. There can be little doubt that the backbone of the extreme activists of 66-73 was derived from the rural population.

141a. LXIX, 14.

142. CIG 4033, 4034: διὰ τὴν κίνησιν τὴν Ἰουδαικήν. Cf. Dio LXIX, 13: πάσης ὡς εἰπεῖν κινουμένης ἐπὶ τούτῳ τῆς οἰκουμένης.

143. Polyb. III, 4, 12; Thuc. III, 75.

144. Cf. Arist. Polit., 1268b 27: τὸ κινεῖν τοὺς πατρίους νόμους.

145. CIL XVI, Dip. 33. But it appears that the Cohors I Lusitanorum serving in Pannonia in 85 was another unit: see Vermes, Millar, op. cit., I, p. 515, n. 12.

146. For the date of his Judaean governorship, Smallwood, JRS LII, 1962, pp. 131

147. Hegesippus ap. Eus. HE, III, 32.

148. Tacitus, I, 1958, p. 222, n. 5.

149. Yadin, IEJ XVII, 1967, p. 45. Izaak points out that the paving of the Via Traiana was begun in the same year.

149a. A newly published inscription from Ephesus (D. Knibbe, Jahresheft des Oesterreichen archaologishen Instituts, 12, 1968-71, cols. 32-39, fig. 9; AE 1972 (1975), p. 178, no. 577), may confirm the occurrence of disorders in the country during Falco's governorship, and even indicate one of the centres affected. It is a dedication in his honour set up by the delegates of the city of Flavia Neapolis (Φλαουιέων Νεαπολιτῶν Σαμαρέων), who had travelled to Ephesus expressly for the purpose; it calls Falco σωτὴρ καὶ εὐεργέτης.

150. JQR LIV, 1963, p. 111.

151. BASOR LXXXVIII, 1942, pp. 10 sqq.

152. BJ IV, 467.

153. BJ II, 458; 480.

154. The decorations on the synagogue fragments included the seven-branched candelabrum, which is virtually lacking in Jewish architectural ornament till after 70. It occurs on Jewish lamps at Cyrene before 115 (IEJ VII, 1957, pp. 154 sqq.; S. Stucchi, Cirene 1957-1966, 1967, p. 163), and on lamps in south-west Judaea prior to the Second Revolt (V. Sussmann, Ornamented Jewish Oil Lamps, 1972 (Heb.), chap. iii, pp. 31-2).

154a. PEQ 1966, p. 96 (1st-century dating); IEJ XIII, 1963, p. 121; XVII, 1967, p. 46. For doubts and criticisms, Bowersock, JRS LXI, 1971, p. 225, and see below.

155. IEJ XVII, 1967, p. 54.

156. 'Atiqot, II, 1959, p. 146; IEJ XIII, 1963, p. 122; PEQ 1969, p. 11.

157. Applebaum, Gihon, Israel and her Vicinity in the Roman and Byzantine Periods, 1967, pp. 47-8.

158. Cf. Note 154a.

159. ILS 2487, line 5.

160. A. Negev IEJ XXI, 1971, p. 124, but without the text. The accompanying epitaph of a man of I Augusta Thracum equitata (ibid.) has been dated by J. C. Mann (IEJ XIX, 1969, p. 211) shortly before or after the annexation of Provincia Arabia.

161. SEG VIII, 345, Wadi Tuweibe. For another inscription, probably to be connected with the legion, in southern Sinai, Rothenberg in Roman Frontier Studies 1967, 1971, p. 223, n. 52.

162. Cat. of Greek Papyri, The Rylands Library, ed. Hunt, p. 237.

163. Alon, op. cit., II, p. 7.

164. A third document (BGU VII, 1564), dated to 138, has been brought into connection with the preceding papyrus (Schehl, Hermes, XLV, 1930, pp. 173 sqq.). As it records the receipt of clothing at Philadelphia, Egypt, for troops in Cappadocia, probably concentrated, in Schehl's view, in response to a Parthian threat, this may also be the explanation of the despatch of clothing to troops in Judaea in 128. The Parthian threat, however, more probably belongs to the year 123/4 (cf. SHA, Had. XII, 8), and in any case neither document appears to me to be relevant to the Jewish revolt.

165. Op. cit., II, p. 1.

166. Mid. Lam. Rab., III, 14.

167. B. Niddah, 61a.

168. R. Kahana was a pupil of R. Ele'azar ben Hyrcanus, a contemporary of R. 'Aqiva.

169. Jer. Yebamot, II, 11, 4a.

170. Collected by Alon, op. cit., II, p. 3.

171. B. Lifschitz, Latomus, XIX, 1960, pp. 110-111.

171a. Seen by myself; for the identification of the legate's name we have to thank B. Izaak, secretary of the Israel Committee of the International Commission for Roman Milestones, to whom I am also grateful for the full text concerned. The stone is no. 395 of the Israel Milestone Committee's record.

172. LXIX, 12-14.

173. For this reason I find it hard to regard as definitive Keppie's suggestion (Latomus, XXXII, 1973, p. 860; cf. Bowersock, JRS LXI, 1971, p. 233), that VI Ferrata had reached Arabia permanently by 125. Whatever the case, the move to Caparcotna could hardly have been made till three or four years later.

174. Tos. Ber. II, 13.

175. B. Yoma 11a. The incident is related by R. Judah ben Ilai (A.D. 140-165). A mezuzah is a small receptacle containing a parchment on which the Ten Commandments are inscribed; it is attached to the doorposts of the Jewish dwelling.

176. ILS 2381 (of Legion III Augusta at Lambaesis).

177. M. Bekh. V, 3.

178. The connection between ethnology and political intelligence work has been well demonstrated by Rudyard Kipling in his novel Kim. The link between archaeology and that branch is represented by E. T. Lawrence.

179. Sif. Deut., para. 143, p. 344; Jer. BQ IV, 4a. For intelligence supervision of a Greek religious centre under Hadrian, cf. ILS 9473, a frumentarius engaged in building (!) at Delphi, awarded citizenship by the Demiurgi.

180. Was Julian making a side-allusion to Hadrian's secret police when he described him (Autok. 311) as πολυπραγμόνων τὰ ἀπόρρητα?

181. See Rostovtzeff, SEHRE II, p. 738, n. 17.

182. Eus. HE, VI, 40.

183. B. Reynolds, JRS, XIII, 1923, p. 181; cf. Aur. Vict., de Caes., 13, 5.

183a. The frumentarii were nominally concerned with commissariat, but in fact were spies and secret agents.

184. Krauss, Griechische u. Lateinische Lehnwörte, II, 1899, p. 409, sv. speculator, speculatria.

185. For additional material on the speculatores, see Schürer, GJV, Eng. trans., I, ii (1890), pp. 62-3. The word occurs in Mark 6: 27, where a speculator executes John the Baptist; I assume that the usage is post-70.

186. Tos. Betzah, II, 6 etc. Cf. Safrai in Rom. Front. Stud. 1967, p. 225.

186a. Mid. Tannaim, p. 224.

187. Note 186.

188. PEFQS 1895, p. 136, no. 62: a quaestionariis - there were several; they were attached to h.q. as professional torturers.

189. Mid. Lam. Rab., I, 17.

190. Murabba'at, p. 125, no. 24B.

190a. I am indebted to Professor Y. Yadin for drawing my attention to this error.

191. Seder'Olam Rabba (Neubauer), II, p. 66; Rattner, p. 145.

192. J. Vogt, Alexandrinische Münzen, I, 1924, p. 103; cf. Schehl, Hermes, LXV, 1930, p. 182.

193. On the evidence of the discharge diploma Dacia, VII-VIII, 1937, pp. 333-4 = AE 44, no. 58 (AD 110).

194. JQR XVI, 1904, pp. 143 sqq.: Die Schauplatz der Bar Kochbakreiges und die auf diesen bezogenen jüdischen Nachtrichten.

195. Yeivin, op. cit., pp. 62 sqq.

196. Jer. Ta'an. IV, 8, 69a; Mid. Lam. Rab. II, 5 (19).

197. Kabul (Chabulon), BJ II, 503; Migdal (Tarichaeae), ibid., III, 485 sqq.

198. Alon, op.cit., II, pp. 19 sqq.

199. Ibid., p. 21.

200. According to Hill, Brit. Mus. Cat., Greek Coins of Pal., 1914, p. xii, under Elegabalus. But the titles ἱερὰ αὐτόνομος under Pius (ibid., p. 3, no. 21) would be sufficient to establish loyalty under Hadrian.

201. Jerome's location of the rebellion (De nat. dom., Morin, 396-397) in Galilee, as Alon remarked (op. cit., II, p. 22), was probably an error induced by the Jewish concentration in Galilee in his own time.

202. M. Peah, VII, 1; Jer. Peah, VII, 1, 20a.

203. CIL III, 12091.

204. QDAP VIII, 1939, p. 57.

205. Arch. News, XXX, 1969, p. 11, and see below p. 31.

206. A. Oppenheimer, Galilee during the Rebellion of Bar Kokhba: Collected Sources: The Roman Period in Israel, pub. The Dept. of Local Studies of the Qibbutz Movement, 1973 (Heb.), pp. 227 sqq.

206a. The problem of whether the Samaritans took an active part in the rising seems at the moment insoluble. The presence of Roman military units at Samaria-Sebaste during the war (Harvard Exped. to Samaria, 1908-1910, I, 1924, p. 20, no. 30, and here p. 45 ; CIL III, 2, 13589; HTR 1909, pp. 111 sqq.) could be interpreted both in favour of such participation and against it. The relevant Samaritan sources, published and discussed in Hebrew by Professor S. Yeivin, both affirm and deny participation (The War of Bar Kokhba,² 1952, pp. 170 sqq.). Professor Yeivin thinks that the Samaritans probably rebelled, but changed sides later. One recent study of the archaeology of an earlier period, however, may throw light on the degree of reliability of Samaritan documents. E. Stern, in The Material Culture of the Land of the Bible in the Persian Period, 1973, (Heb.) p. 251, concludes from the evidence of destruction about the year 332 BC at various sites in the north of the country, that Samaria and the north were closely allied with Tyre during Alexander the Great's siege of that city. This directly discredits Josephus' information (Ant. XI, 321) (doubtless derived from a Samaritan source) that Sanballat, the Samaritan high priest, had come to assist Alexander at Tyre with 6,000 troops; this claim is further disproved by the evidence of the Wadi Dalya documents (HTR 59, 1966, p. 201). On the attitude of the Samaritans to the Second Revolt, therefore, it would be wise to withold judgment till more definite evidence is available.

207. In conversation with the writer.

208. It should however be noted that a coin of Ben Kosba is reliably recorded as having been found at Tzippori (Sepphoris) by the Encyclopedea of Excavations, II, 1970, p. 498 (Heb.); it bore the find-number D20 and was re-examined by the author of the relevant article, the late Professor Avi-Yonah. It was originally assigned to the first revolt (Waterman, Excavs. at Sepphoris, 1937, p. 40). It was found in the Roman villa partly excavated by Waterman and Manasseh.

209. I am indebted to Mr. A. Kindler of the Museum Ha-Aretz, Tel Aviv, for the above survey and details. See also Kindler, The Dating and Meaning of Ancient Jewish Coins and Symbols, Numismatic Studies and Researches, II, Israel Numismatic Society, 1958, pp. 62 sqq.; The Coinage of the Bar Kokhba War. Cf. ibid., Kadman, pp. 102-3, and Kindler, Coins in Palestine through the Ages, 1973, p. 26. For a general biography of Ben Kosba's coinage, Vermes, Millar, Hist. of the Jewish People, I, p. 26.

210. QDAP II, 1932/3, p. 120; Avi-Yonah, Hist. Geografit shel Eretz Yisrael, 1962, (Heb.), p. 86.

211. QDAP XII, 1947/8, pp. 96 (no. 13) - 101 sq.

212. Luria, King Yannai, p. 47.

213. RétJ, I, 1880, p. 48; CIL VIII (ii), 8934.

214. Britain and the Roman Army, 1953, p. 24.

215. S. Cornelius Dexter, of the first inscription, prefect of the Syrian fleet in the war, had previously commanded the Ala Gemina Augusta Colonorum, part of which had originated in the Jewish mounted archers from Babylonia settled in Bashan by Herod. (See the writer, Studies in the Hist. of the Jewish People and the Land of Israel, I, Haifa University, 1970, pp. 79 sqq.) (Heb. , Eng. résumé.) Dexter may have been selected for his command under Hadrian because of his familiarity with oriental, even Jewish troops, and "combined" (i.e. landing) operations may have been involved. Col. Galili, on the other hand, has suggested to me the possibility that the operations concerned took place on the Dead Sea.

216. B. Mazar, Eretz Yisrael, I, 1951, pp. 69-70.

217. The area doubtless reverted to the fiscus (it was geographically within the Har ha-Melekh area); one may observe that the ruined city would have made an ideal hide-out, and note the traditional nexus between the Har ha-Melekh and the Second Revolt. It is further worth noting Strabo's record (XVI, 759) that in Augustus' reign Jewish pirates held both the Sharon (ὁ δρυμός) and the Carmel. The Roman road recently traced from Caesarea to Antipatris (PEQ 1973, pp. 91-99) is shown by milestones to have been "adopted" by the Roman authorities in the later 2nd or 3rd century, but it was probably used in 66 by Cestius Gallus, later by Vespasian, and as it cut across the forest-country it may represent operations aimed at clearing this tract of dissident Jewish elements.

218. Arch. News of the Govt. Dept. of Antiquities, XVII, 1967, p. 18. See below, p. 29.

219. For the Jewish population of Mount Carmel in the 1st century BC, cf. Josephus, Ant. XIV, 334, also n. 217.

219a. Benoit et al., Murabba'at, p. 125, no. 24B, dated to Year 2 of the Redemption of Israel. Hillel ben Garis is here named as tenant (line 6).

220. Davar, 2nd May, 1972.

221. Mid. Lam. Rab. II, 19: Kefar Bish, Kefar Shiḥelayyim, Kefar Dikhrin.

221a. V. Sussman, op. cit., pp. 32-3.

222. LXIX, 12, 2-14.

223. The problem of the reliability of Dio's figures is discussed on p. 34.

223a. V. Sussman, op. cit., pp. 32-3.

223b. S. Applebaum, JGAC, (Heb.-Eng. résumé) 1969, pp. 205-209, developing IEJ VII 1957, pp. 154 sqq. Cf. Eretz Yisrael VI, 1961, pp. 73 sqq. (Heb.-Eng. résumé).

224. JRS XII, 1922, p. 66.

225. BGU I, 140.

226. CIL VI, 3492a, b; ILS 2288.

227. Harnack, Texte u. Untersuchungen der altchristlichen Literatur, 1882, 4, 44; Abel, Hist. de la Paléstine, II, 1952, p. 93, n. 1.

228. E.g. CAH XI, 1936, p. 313; Collingwood, Myres, Roman Britain and the English Settlements, 1937, pp. 128-9, where Collingwood opposed Ritterling's suggestion (PW XII, 2, sv. Legio, cols. 1668-9), that the legion was wiped out at a later date.

229. E. B. Birley in Butler, (ed.), Soldier and Civilian in Roman Yorkshire, 1971, pp. 71 sqq.; cf. idem. Britain and the Roman Army, 1953, pp. 25-8.

230. CIL X, 1769.

231. Loc. cit.

232. LXXI, 2, 1.

233. CIL VI, 3492, a, b.

234. The Roman Legions, 1928, p. 163.

235. Quid? avo vestro imperium obtinente, quantum militum ab Judaeis, quantum ab Britannis caesum. Fronto's letter to Antoninus Pius, AD 162, - Haines, II, p. 22.

236. Chiron, II, 1972, p. 459 sqq.

237. Ibid., p. 449 sqq.

238. Hist. Rom., Syr., 50: Οὐεσπασιανὸς αὖθις οἰκισθεῖσαν κατέσκαψε καὶ Ἁδριανὸς αὖθις ἐπ'ἐμοῦ - all the more impressive because the building of Aelia had begun before the outbreak of 132. Cf. Eus. Dem. Evan. VI, 18. 10 - PG XXII, 453 (ad Zech. 14:2): τὸν λοιπὸν τῆς πόλεως μέρος ἥμισυ πολιορκηθὲν αὖθις ἐξελαύνεται ὡς ἐξ ἐκείνου καὶ ἐς δεῦρο πάμπαν ἄβατον αὐτοῖς γένεσθαι τὸν τόπον.

239. Kindler, Coins in Palestine, p. 26.

240. Ibid.

241. For the information on the present results of the excavations I am indebted to Professor B. Mazar and Mr. M. Ben Dov. I take the liberty of citing the relevant portion of Professor Mazar's communication. "The period of 70-135 CE and that of the Second Revolt are represented in our excavations only slightly and by a very brief finds-list. Remains of flooring and channels in the vicinity of the south-west corner of the Temple Mount can be ascribed to this period. Among the finds may be mentioned coins from Vespasian to Hadrian (inter alia, coins inscribed 'Judaea capta' and numerous Nabataean coins), also one solitary coin of Bar Kokhba, of Year 2, found in the street along the south Temple wall, of the lowest and earliest phase of the Roman period... A small number of lamps, complete or fragmentary, characteristic of this period, was also found. Recently a problem has arisen concerning a group of pottery in one of the loci which can be ascribed to the period before the building of Aelia Capitolina. Datable to the late 'seventies is a fragment of column with a Latin inscription (Qadmoniot, V, 1972, 3-4, p. 83). As to the Roman structures and the numerous finds of tiles and bricks with stamps of the Tenth Legion, pottery, bronzes, coins, etc. - all belong explicitly to the period of Aelia Capitolina after the time of Bar Kokhba." Since the above information was furnished, Professor Mazar reports that one more coin of Ben Kosba has come to light in the area.

242. The participation of this legion in the Jewish war is independently attested by an inscription of Caesarea (A. Negev, Arch. News, VII, 1961, p. 2).

242a. RB 1904, pp. 94 sqq.

243. It is very difficult to accept the evidence advanced by J. Meyshan (PEQ 1958, pp. 19 sqq.) for the presence at Jerusalem at this date of the legion V Macedonica, to which he attributes the recapture of the city. The evidence is that of a "founder" coin of Aelia with the legion's name in abbreviated form (LE V) inscribed on a vexillum. It seems

altogether probable, provided that this inscription has been correctly read, that we are faced with an error for "LE X".

244. Avi-Yonah, Hist. Geog. shel Eretz Yisrael,³ 1962, in his appendix pp. 179-190, records a number of alleged Roman camps and forts among the chief remains of the Mishnaic and talmudic periods. Most of these are derived from the reports of earlier observers, and a re-examination of the sites concerned (in so far as they are still extant) is desirable before any conclusions can be based upon them.

245. Seeck, Oriens, XXXIV.

246. See Gihon ap. Applebaum, Gihon, Israel and her Vicinity, pp. 35 sqq.; pp. 45-6 (Arad); Fritz, ZDPV 89, 1973, pp. 54 sqq.; (Tell es-Saba'); Gihon, Saalburger Jahrbuch, XXXI, 1974, pp. 16 sqq. (Tzafit), and now Gihon, Eretz Yisrael, XII, (Glueck Memorial Vol.), 1975, pp. 149-166: The Sites of the Limes in the Negev.

247. Tos. Shabb. XIII, 9.

248. E.g. IEJ XVI, 1966, pp. 256 sqq.; Jalabert, Mouterde, Inscrs. grecques et romaines de la Syrie, 1929-67, 1188 etc.

249. Liddel and Scott,⁹ 1940, ad voc.

250. Vita, 104.

251. Ibid., 394.

251a. Vita, 411.

252. BJ III, 59.

252a. See n. 58.

253. QDAP XII, 1946, p. 91.

254. Tell el-Mutesellim, I, Tafeln, 1908, Map 1.

255. Hieron. PL XXV, 1589; Hierocles, Synecdemesis, 720, 10.

256. Arch. News XVII, 1966, p. 18, and personal communication from Dr. Y. Algabish, here cited in the text.

257. IEJ XVII, 1967, pp. 43 sqq. Cf. I. A. Richmond, JRS LII, 1962, pp. 150-151 and fig. 7.

258. These platforms, which vary in size, appear to measure about five metres in depth by $2\frac{1}{2}$-five metres in width. Baatz (Bonn.Jb 166, p. 199) gives the minimal dimensions for the emplacement of a light artillery piece as 3 x 3.5 metres.

259. D. Baatz, Bonn. Jb. 1966, pp. 194 sqq. and especially pp. 197-8.

259a. Avi-Yonah, Geog. Hist. pp. 143-4; Judith 4:4.

260. Yadin, Polotzky, BIES XXVI, 1962, p. 239.

261. Arch. News XIII, 1965, p. 3.

262. J. Kelso, D. C. Baramki, Excavations at New Testament Jericho and Khirbet Anetla, 1955, (AASOR XXIX-XXX), 1949-51, p. 8.

263. R. J. Ball, PEQ 1966/7, pp. 163-165.

263a. An ex-centurion, T. Flavius Ouales, of an unknown cohort (presumably equitata) buried his wife at Beth Nattif between Eleutheropolis and Bethar, in or after the Flavian period (IGR III, 1207); as a second inscription by him (ibid. 1206) is set up ἐν τοῖς ἰδίοις, he and his family were settled here, hence we cannot be sure of the presence of a fort. The veteran's name looks Palmyrene.

263c. IEJ XXIV, 1974, pp. 160 sqq.

263d. Arch. News LIV-LV, 1975, p. 22.

264. BJ III, 12. How the presence of this force is to be reconciled with Ascalon's status as a civitas foederata is another question.

265. Ant. XIX, 364.

266. Jos. Vita, 115.

267. BJ III, 429-430.

267a. Ibid. IV, 486.

268. Ibid.

269. Tell Saba' - see n. 246; Moleatha (Tell el-Milik) cf. Alt. PJb 1930, p. 58 and n. 3. The excavations here have not been reported, but see Gihon, Eretz Yisrael, XII, 1975, p. 153.

270. For all these, see Schalit, King Herod, pp. 172-207 (Heb.).

270a. BJ II, 408.

270b. CIL XVI, no. 33.

271. Judging by legionary evidence at Abbu Gosh (Qiriat Ye'arim) (Abel, RB 1925, p. 580; 1934, p. 351), and Jaffa, X Fretensis may have been responsible for securing its line of communication with the port. The V Macedonica at Emmaus was not stationed there permanently.

272. Not identical with the Cohors I Lusitanorum stationed in Pannonia according to Diploma XVII (CIL. XVI, no. 31).

273. Lesquier, L'armée romain de l'Egypte, 1918, p. 92.

274. Tos. Betzah, II, 6; Mid. Lam. Rab. II, 5 (19); B. Gitt. 55b; Jer. Ta'anit, IV, 8, 69a.

275. Cf. what has been said above on the Roman intelligence service.

276. Kromayer, Veith, Heerwesen und Kriegführung der Griechen und Römer, 1928, pp. 544-546.

277. ILS 2262, 2265; cf. Suet. Domit., VII, 2.

278. Limesforschungen, 4, 1962, p. 87.

279. Jour. Chester Arch. Soc., XXXVIII, 1951, p. 19.

280. RIB 557.

281. The presence of a naval unit has also been suggested - Starr, The Roman Imperial Navy, 31 BC-AD 324, 1941, p. 165, n. 105.

282. Nash-Williams, Jarrett, The Roman Frontier in Wales,² 1969, p. 31.

283. Der römische Limes in Oesterreich, III.

284. JRS LI, 1961, pp. 158-160.

285. Röm. Limes in Oester., XV.

286. R. Cagnat, L'armée romaine d'Afrique, 1912, pp. 526 sqq. But see Syme, Tacitus, I, p. 222, n. 4 on the date AD 81 for reconstruction.

287. RB 1931, pp. 292-4; cf. SHA, Had., V, 5, 8.

288. Nash-Williams, Jarrett, op. cit., p. 17.

289. CIL XVI, no. 87.

290. The War of Bar Kokhba, 1946, p. 176.

291. II, 5 (20).

292. PW XV, 1932, col. 1815, sv. Minucius (11).

293. Schürer GJV I, 1901, pp. 674-5, n. 72. F. Millar, The Study of Cassius Dio, 1964, p. 62, thinks that a "coherent source seems to underlie Dio's account" (of the Jewish revolt of 132-5). He sees Hadrian's reports to the Senate as a possible authority.

294. M. Kokhbi (ed.), Archaeological Survey of Judaea, Samaria and the Golan, 1967-1968, 1972.

294a. Essays and Studies in the Lore of the Holy Lands, 1963, p. 121 (Heb.).

294b. Papers in Economic Prehistory, ed. Higgs, 1972, p. 179.

294c. JQR XXXIV, 1943-4, pp. 62-3.

295. For the despatch of one Syrian legion to Judaea under the Syrian legate Publicius Marcellinus, CIG. 4033 (= IGR III, 174). Although the inscription can be taken to imply the despatch also of XVI Flavia Firma, which has been assumed by some scholars to have been in Syria at the time, I know of no evidence of this, nor is there anything to show that the legion was present in Syria under Hadrian. The earliest evidence for the legion's presence in Syria after Trajan appears to be ILS 9115, dated to 149.

296. The suggestion of Professor Birley in a conversation with me. A legionary building inscription from the aqueduct north of Caesarea Maritima, found in 1963 (A. Negev, Arch. News, VII, 1963, pp. 1-2) was only partly legible and might have belonged either to the VI Ferrata or to the XXII Deioteriana. Professor Negev thought that the name and number of the legion recorded had perhaps been erased. If this were correct, we should know that this was XXII Deioteriana, also that the legion had been some time in Judaea before it became engaged in critical action; further that it was disbanded in disgrace. Unfortunately there is no certainty.

297. Ant. XVII, 282.

298. BJ II, 541-554.

299. BJ II, 546-550.

300. Copyright Harvard University Press; from Josephus, The Jewish War II, pp. 547-555, trans. H. St.J. Thackeray.

301. "Marching along a watershed...has many advantages...." P. Stibbs, an officer of Orde Wingate's Chindits, in reference to the Chindwin campaign of 1943, as cited by C. Sykes, Orde Wingate, 1959, p. 396, from P. Stibbe, Return from Burma.

302. Josephus' source may have been Roman, condensing accounts describing different stages of the action.

303. BJ II, 499-501.

304. I Macc. iii, 16-24. I owe these points to Dr. B. Bar Kokhba, who has made a close study of the ground of the Maccabean campaigns as a whole.

305. BJ II, 573.

306. BJ III, 289-306.

307. As a further instructive analogy may be cited the repulse of Titus from the built-up area of Jerusalem after breaching the second wall of the city; despite the use of archers to check the Jews advancing down the streets, his troops were forced to evacuate the Upper City (BJ V, 336-341).

308. BJ IV, 5 sqq.

309. Cf. especially Josephus' graphic account in BJ IV, 21-29, which has every appearance of authenticity. The site has recently been re-identified on the basis of Josephus' topographical account; its location at Tell Aḥdab near Jemaleh is impossible in terms of BJ IV, 1. The new site is as-Salem south-east of Bir Qaruah, Israel grid 256.4/219.5.

310. PJb. XXVII, 1931, pp. 111 sqq; Jüdische Wälde.

310a. For these identifications I am indebted to Professor A. Horowitz and Mrs. M. Gersonde of the Archaeological Institute of Tel Aviv University.

311. BJ VI, 151.

312. Loc. cit., pp. 115-120.

313. Hist., II, 42.

314. BJ III, 115-6.

315. The analogous layout of some developed British Early Iron Age hillforts with their successively rising concentric ramparts will come to mind, although these were not always or necessarily connected with sling warfare. Maiden Castle, nevertheless, possesses slingers' platforms and graded ramparts, built to command those lower than themselves. (L. Rivet ap. Frere, Problems of the Iron Age in Southern Britain, 1960, p. 31). I am indebted to Professor Rivet for advice on this point.

316. Ectaxis, XVI, 3.

317. The War Scroll, in its account of the tactics and formation of the messianic army, refers on a number of occasions to cavalry (Y. Yadin,

The Scroll of the War of the Sons of Light against the Sons of Darkness, 1955 (Heb.), Index). Mounted archers are mentioned in X [6], 15. This is a partly restored paragraph, but the restoration is almost certainly correct, since the passage as a whole deals with cavalry. The Jews are likely to have made acquaintance with this form of combat earliest during the Armenian invasion of Tigranes (Ant. XIII, 419); but they are more likely to have seen it in 40 BCE, when the Parthian Pacorus attacked Judaea and reached Idumaea (Ant. XIV, 353). The presence of the Babylonian Jew Zamaris, captain of mounted archers in Syria, dated from 23 BC (Ant. XVII, 23 sq.). Dr. Bar Kokhba has noted the presence of cavalry among the forces of Judah the Maccabee, most suggestive being the presence of a trooper, Τουβεινος (according to an amendment of the text of II Macc. xii, 35) at Marissa. The only hint of the participation of mounted men in Ben Kosba's forces is the famous tradition according to which the scholars suggest to Ben Kosba that instead of compelling his men to amputate a finger as a test of endurance, he select them according to their ability to uproot a cedar (Mid. Lam. Rab. II, 5 (19)).

318. Cf. J. W. Eadie, JRS LVII, 1967, pp. 166 sqq.

319. E.g. Caesar, B. Civ. III, 4, 3, 5.

320. For a comprehensive list, H. Van de Weerd, P. Lambrechts, Laureae Aquincenses, I, 1938, pp. 230 sqq.

321. Ibid., p. 231.

322. BJ II, 500, 501.

323. Die Konskriptionsordnung, Gesammelte Schriften, VI, 1910, pp. 103 sqq.

324. Zur angeblichen Barbarisierung der römischen Heeres durch die Verbände der Numeri, Historia, I, 1950, pp. 389 sqq.

325. Die Kaiserliche Beamte und Truppenkörpe in römischen Deutschland unter dem Prinzipat, 1932, pp. 233 sqq.

326. Yale Classical Studies VI, 1939, pp. 73 sqq.; cf. PW, 2, XVII, cols. 327-341.

327. BRGK 45, 1964, pp. 133 sqq.: Die fremden Truppen im römischen Heer des Prinzipates.

328. I retain the German term in order to avoid confusion between this type of unit and the auxilia.

329. Callies, loc. cit., pp. 169-170.

330. Ibid., pp. 181-2.

331. Ibid., pp. 205 sqq.

332. This development has nothing to do with the old theory that by the 2nd century the auxilia had become assimilated in tactics and armament to the legions. (Von Domaczewski, Der Religion des römischen Heeres, 1895, p. 29, n. 124; Kromayer, Veith, Heerwesen, p. 524; Delbrück, Gesch. der Kriegskunst, II, 1920, pp. 168 sqq.; 495. This view does not appear to be substantiated; cf. Cheesman, Auxilia of the Roman Army, 1914, pp. 130-132; Couissin, Les armes romaines, 1926, pp. 359 sqq.

333. Saalburg Jb., XXV, 1968, pp. 185 sqq.; Roman Frontier Studies 1967, 1973, pp. 98-101; cf. Fabricius, Festschr. d. Univ. Freiburg, 1902, pp. 291-3.

334. SHA, Ant. Pius, V, 4.

335. Stein, Kais. Beamten, p. 266; Cheesman, Auxilia, p. 88; von Domaczewski, Die Rangordnung des röm. Heeres, Bonn. Jb., 117, 1908, pp. 60-61; Rowell, PW XVII, 1937, sv. Numerus, cols. 1339, 1340.

336. Loc. cit., p. 208.

337. Loc. cit., p. 214.

338. Frontinus, Strateg. I, 3, 10; II, 3, 23; Fabricius, ORL LII, 1935, pp. 43 sq.; Schoenberger, JRS LIX, 1969, p. 158; Ritterling, Jahresheft Oest. Arch. Inst., VII, 1904, pp. 25 sq.

339. Syme, CAH XI, 1936, p. 165.

340. This is confirmed by reference to Westermann, Lexikon der Geographie, 1970, IV, pp. 962-3, sv. Wetterau, where it is stated that the agricultural importance of the area lies in its immense cover of diluvial loess. According to the same source, however, the high land of the west Vogelsberg to the east of the Wetterau (ibid., III, p. 851, sv.) is forested, while the Upper Taunus to the west of the Wetterau is predominantly a forest tract. (ibid., IV, p. 535, sv.).

341. Strategemata, II, 3.23.

342. Ibid., I, 3.10.

342a. Ems, Arbach, Hunzel, Holzhausen, Kemel, Zugmantel, Heftrich, Feldberg, Kapersburg. - Schoenberger, Germania, XXV, 1937, p. 118, Abb. 1.

343. Schleiermacher, Die römische Limes in Deutschland,³ 1967, p. 218; Schoenberger, JRS LIX, 1969, pp. 168-9.

344. Die röm. Limes in Deutschland, p. 212.

345. Callies, Die fremden Truppen, BRGK 45, p. 216; Stein, Kais. Beamten, pp. 254, 260.

346. A single detail may adequately illustrate the correctness of this view. The garrison of Hadrian's Wall included only one battalion of archers, whose presence clearly did not reflect an arbitrary decision that one individual fort should be defended by bowmen. The archer unit was present in order to furnish a necessary component of task forces despatched northward on offensive missions. I assume that in Germany the Cohors I Damascenorum MES performed a similar rôle, its station at Friedburg being ideally placed for the exploitation of interior lines. For a restatement of the offensive rôle of the forces on Hadrian's Wall, cf. Breeze, Dobson, Britannia, III, 1972, pp. 192 sqq.; Hadrian's Wall: Some Problems.

347. Stein, op.cit., p. 240; Cheesman, Auxilia, p. 112; W. Wagner, Die Dislokation der römischen Auxiliarformationen in den Provinzen Noricum, Pannonien, Moesien und Dakien von Augustus bis Gallienus, 1938, pp. 203, 209, 214; Rowell, PW XVII, col. 1339; von Domaczewski, Rangordnung (n. 335), p. 59.

348. In Africa also the evidence does not appear to be in favour of the defensive rôle of numeri. They took over the duties of Legion III Augusta in the protection of the western scarp of the Aures Mountains. (Callies, loc.cit., p. 209).

349. Richmond, JRS LII, 1962, p. 152.

350. Cf. the mixed cavalry and legionary force at Hod Hill, Dorset, (Britain), in the area of Vespasian's command (Suet. Vesp., 4) - Richmond, Hod Hill, II, 1968, pp. 76, 122.

350a. CIL VI, 1523; XII, 2230.

351. RB 1894, p. 614; QDAP VIII, 1939, p. 57, no. 2.

352. CIL X, 3733 = ILS 2083; cf. Vermes, Millar, Hist. Jew. People, I, p. 548 n. 150; Arch. News, VII, 1964, p. 2 - Caesarea.

353. CIL VI, 1523.

354. CIL XIV, 3610.

355. RB 1904, pp. 94 sqq.

355a. RB 1894, p. 614; PW XII, 2, col. 1578.

356. RB XXV, p. 421.

356a. Arch. Survey of Judaea etc., p. 25, map 2.

357. CIL XVI, no. 33.

358. CIL XVI, no. 87.

359. JRS LIX, 1969, p. 169; Limesforschungen, 2, 1962, p. 131; Radnóti, Germania, LXXIX, 1961, pp. 114-115.

360. W. Wagner, op.cit., (n. 347), pp. 153, 170, 196, 231 sqq.

361. The units recorded in CIL III, 600 (= CIL III, 14203, 35), found also in a Syrian diploma of AD 157, were previously believed to have participated in Trajan's Parthian campaigns and hence to have been candidates for the Jewish war of Hadrian (Cheesman, Auxil., p. 156). But it has since been shown by Borman that at least one of the units concerned was not transferred to the east before AD 138, and they served, apparently, in the Parthian expedition of L. Verus. (See ad CIL XVI, no. 106; Borman, Ritterling, Jb Oest. Arch. Inst., III, pp. 23 sqq.).

362. Harvard Excavations at Samaria, I, 1924, p. 20, no. 30; pp. 231 sq.; 176, fig. 91; V. de Weerd, Ant. Class., VII, 1938, pp. 81 sqq.; Alfoldi, ibid., XVII, 1948, pp. 13 sqq.; Cheesman, Aux., p. 76.

363. See Alföldi, loc.cit., p. 16.

364. But see above, p. 45.

365. E. Birley, Carnuntina, III, 1956, p. 27.

366. Clearly the recorded number of cavalry units is too low and there must in fact have been more.

367. This distribution indeed suggests that the final advance to Jerusalem and Bethar was from the north along the ridgeway. (Cf. Yeivin, The War of Bar Kokhba, p. 92). The southern approach was in Jewish hands; the country to the west, as already indicated, a tactical risk; the northerly approach, though not without its dangers (cf. I Macc., 3, 10-11) is more equable. For further evidence bearing on the limits of the war, see here p. 56.

367a. See here n. 487 on the date of Hadrian's consultation of Apollonius concerning artillery for use against hill-positions.

368. For the defeat of an enemy in a built-up area by seizure of the housetops, compare the successful operations of Simon the Hasmonean's troops in Antioch (Jos., Ant. XIII, 137-140).

369. AE 1948, no. 148.

370. Callies, loc. cit., pp. 161-3; Wagner, Dislokation, pp. 166 sqq.

371. PW XVII, 1937, Nachträge, col. 2553 (Rowell).

372. ILS 8908; Wagner, Dislokation, p. 203.

373. ILS 9187.

374. CIL VI, 1523 = ILS 1092.

375. PW IIIA^2, 1929, sv. Statius (18), col. 2218. Statius' tribunate of X Gemina belongs to the late years of Hadrian or the early years of Pius.

376. Dip. XXXII, AD 103 = CIL XVI, no. 43; see Nash-Williams, Jarrett, op. cit., p. 15.

377. R. Saxer, Epigrafische Studien: Untersuchungen zu den Vexillationen des römischen Kaiserheeres von Augustus bis Diokletian, 1967, p. 29, no. 51.

378. See here p. 31.

379. Nash-Williams, Jarrett, op. cit., p. 17.

379a. Op. cit.

379b. Britons and the Roman Army, 1964.

379c. Ap. Foster, Daniel, Prehistoric and Early Wales, 1965, especially pp. 126 sqq.

379d. Ap. Culture and Environment, Papers in honour of Sir Cyril Fox, 1966, figs., pp. 57, 58.

379e. Ap. Foster, Daniel, op. cit., pp. 151 sqq.

380. Nash-Williams, Jarrett, op. cit., p. 23, map 5.

381. Although the fort at Carmarthen has probably now been found (JRS LIX, 1969, p. 198; Britannia, I, 1970, p. 270), it is notable that by the early 2nd century Moridunum was a town, later walled - mentioned by Ptolemy (II, 3, 23), but evidently a pagus capital (like Petuaria) and not, so far as is known, with municipal rank. It was known to the Itinerarium Antonini (Iter XII), and therefore still existed at the end of the 2nd century.

381a. Hogg ap. Foster, Daniel, op. cit., p. 128; cf. Appendix I, pp. 133 sqq.

382. Caesaque prope universa gente - Tac. Ag. XVIII, 41.

383. Foster, Daniel, op. cit., figs. 15, 17, Savory's map, reproduced as fig. 18 by Simpson, Britons and the Roman Army, p. 141.

384. The sources are the maps of Daniel, Foster and Savory already referred to. I here omit consideration of the Glamorgan castella, since not enough information is at my disposal to establish their relation to centres of native occupation.

385. Foster, Daniel, op. cit., fig. 17.

386. Culture and Environment, fig. 57.

387. Op. cit., p. 112.

388. Culture and Environment, figs. 57, 58.

389. CBA Research Reports, VII, 1966, Rural Settlement in Roman Britain, p. 32, fig. 2.

390. Trans. and Proc. Birmingham Arch. Soc., LXXXII, 1965, pp. 77-91.

391. Nash-Williams, Jarrett, op. cit., p. 25, fig. 8.

392. From Ireland - Collingwood, Myres, Rom. Brit. and the Eng. Settlements,[2] 1937, pp. 282-3; M. Richards, Jour. Roy. Soc. Antiquaries of Ireland, XC, 1960, pp. 133-162; Anglesey, G. R. J. Jones, Agrarian Hist. of Eng. and Wales, I, ii, 1972, pp. 287, 296.

393. The special mention of Moridunum as the only centre of the Demetae suggests that Ptolemy's Welsh list should be dated c. 120-150. The Ravenna Cosmography contains 14 names attributable to Wales; among the sites of those identifiable, the latest occupied appears to have been abandoned in c. 160. But Ravennas does not mention Moridunum, whose civil town began to develop in the first half of the 2nd century-and see here n. 381.

394. Simpson, op. cit., p. 131; H. N. Savory, Dinorben, 1964, pp. 72 sq. Hogg (CBA Res. Rpt, VII, p. 31) estimated the population of the northwest of the country (Anglesey, Caernarvonshire, Merioneth) at 4,000 in the later Roman period.

395. Not. Dig. (Seeck), Occid., XL, 34. I suspect that this was enrolled from the inhabitants of the western Pagus (Powys) of Viroconium, and could therefore be reckoned with the genuine Welsh mountain population. See J. Morris, The Age of Arthur, 1973, p. 63.

396. Collingwood, Myres, op. cit., pp. 312-3; Morris, op. cit., p. 254.

397. Op. cit., p. 119.

398. Ibid., pp. 173 sq.

399. Professor Avi-Yonah on the basis of restricted archaeological surveys carried out prior to 1947 (Three Historical Memoranda, 1947, pp. 3-16; cf. idem, Essays and Studies in the Lore of the Holy Land, 1964, pp. 114 sqq., especially p. 121) estimated the population of the hill-country of Western Palestine in the late Roman period (i.e. before AD 300) as 1,880,000 souls. For purposes of the present study the population of Galilee must be subtracted from this estimate.

400. Dio LXIX, 14.2: ‘ὥστε πᾶσαν ὀλίγου δεῖν τὴν Ἰουδαίαν ἐρηνωθῆναι.

401. Hieron., Chron., (Schoene), p. 177, ad ann. 2216; cf. SHA Severus, XVI, 7; Abel, Hist. de la Palestine, II, 1952, pp. 151 sq.

402. Arch. Survey of Judaea etc., p. 25, map 2.

403. Arch. News, XXVI, 1968, pp. 27-8.

403a. E.g. F. Koepp, Die Römer in Deutschland, 1926, Abb. 63, 64.

404. Tos. 'Erub., VI, 4.

405. M. Harel, IEJ XVII, 1967, pp. 18 sqq., and especially fig. 1, p. 19. In their hairpin negotiation of grades, causewayed crossings of streambeds, and revetted flanks, these roads resemble example now found by Mr. Shim'on Dar on the south-west slopes of Mount Hermon. Cf. the recorded reduction of an Ituraean hillfort in 4 BC (EE IV, 1881, p. 538). But in the Ḥermon region these roads certainly also served the agricultural settlements.

406. Benoit et al., Murabba'at, p. 163, no. 45.

407. Yadin, Jud. Des. Stud.; The Finds from the Bar Kokhba Period, pp. 11-14 and fig. 3.

407a. Cf. Newstead, Scotland - J. Curle, A Roman Frontier Post and its People, 1911, pp. 74-5. The fort between Jericho and Ramallah, on the north edge of the area, is larger than the rest (0.96 hectare).

408. Agadat Cant. (Schechter, Buber), ad VI,9.

409. Giḥon, Bonn. Jb, 171, 1971, pp. 386 sqq.

410. Naḥal Hever and its Roman camp (above, n. 407), likewise the camp at the "Cave of Horror" ('Atiqot, III, 1966, pp. 152, 153).

411. Y. Aharoni, 'Atiquot, III, pp. 159, 161.

412. I, 17.

413. P. Oxy. 1205; QDAP V, 1925, p. 155.

413a. XXXIV, 48.

414. Notable is the discovery of the discharge certificate CIL XVI, no. 87 of AD 139 (no. CIX) at Fiq, a short distance east of Susita, suggesting settlement of veteran auxiliary troops in the vicinity not long after the Jewish war.

415. Tos. Ma'as. Shen. I, 6.

416. E.g. Benoit et al., Murabba'at, p. 48, nos. 114, 117; BIES XXV, 1961, pp. 75, no. 4 (Naḥal Tzeelim); ibid., p. 33 (Cave 34).

417. SHA, Pius, V, 4. See M. Smallwood, Latomus XVIII, 1959, pp. 340-341 (dating the rising to 155-163); Weber, CAH XI, p. 337 (after 152).

418. Ann. PG CXI, 987: Fuerunt autem e Iudaeis qui Aegyptum fugerent, alii qui Syriam et in montes et in regionem Algaur.

418a. M Yeb. XVI, 7; see Alon, Researches in Jewish Hist., II, 1958, pp. 93 sqq. (Heb.)

419. Not. Dig. Oriens, XXXIV, 26.

420. Not. Dig., Oriens, XXXIV, 20.

421. Applebaum, Giḥon, Israel and her Vicinity, pp. 46-7; 55.

422. LXIX, 13, 2.

423. S. Frere, Britannia, 1967, p. 139.

424. SHA, Had., XIV, 1.

424a. Downey, Hist. of Antioch, 1961, p. 223, n. 109.

425. SHA, Loeb, ad loc.

426. Loc. cit.

427. Suidas (Adler) IV, 1935, p. 69, no. 809; BMC, Greek Coins, Galatia etc., p. 283, no. 8; ibid., p. 117, no. 19.

428. Herodian, III, 6, 9; Malalas, (Bonn), p. 293; Ulp. Dig. L, xv, 1, 3; Paulus, L, 15, 8, 3.

429. For all these, with sources, Magie, Roman Rule in Asia Minor, I, 1950, pp. 599-601.

430. Augustus and the Greek World, 1965, pp. 101 sqq.

431. SHA, Pius, V, 5.

432. Dio Chrys., Orat. XXXII, 10 (Arnim).

433. See the present author, Scripta Classica Israelica, I, 1974, pp. 116 sqq.: Domitian's Assassination: the Jewish Aspect.

434. Mid. Gen. Rab., 65. 1.

435. Julian, Είς τούς άπαιδ.κύνας 187, 199.

436. 65, 20.

437. CIL III, 12091.

438. For a possible gentile among Ben Kosba's forces, cf. IEJ XI, 1961, p. 46, no. 11 (Thyriss bar Tinianus). Not all the Greek cities surrounding Judaea reacted violently to their Jewish communities in the year 66 and after; notable exceptions were Gerasa, Sidon and Apamea (BJ II, 477-480). The inconsistent behaviour of Antioch and Scythopolis is accountable

partly by the degree of firmness exhibited by the Roman administration, possibly by the presence of conflicting attitudes among the population. Gadara appears (according to Josephus, BJ II, 459) to have been initially attacked by the Jews, yet subsequently (ibid., 478), like Hippos and Tyre, to have put to death only the aggressive Jews and to have confined the rest.

439. Dio (Epit.), LXIX, 12, 2.

440. A. Reifenberg, Coins of the Jews (Heb.), 1947, p. 32; L. Kadman, ap. The Dating and Meaning of Ancient Jewish Coins and Symbols, pp. 102-103.

441. L. Finkelstein, Akiba, 1936 (ed. 1947), p. 215.

442. B. Sota, 49b; J. Ta'an. IV, 8, 69a.

443. V, 7.

444. "Aforetime a persecution was ordained in Judaea, for they possessed a tradition from their fathers that Judah slew Esau, it being written that thy hand shall be upon the neck of thine enemies."

445. Diploma CIL XVI, no. 107 = CIL III, 2, XL.

446. 1 sq. (PG VI, 473, 474): οἱ μετὰ τοῦ Τρύφωνος

447. φυγὼν τὸν νῦν γενόμενον πόλεμον (ib., 473).

448. Ibid.

449. Benoit et al., Murabba'at, II, p. 218, no. 90e ii (Ἑλλῆλος Κυρηναῖ[ος].).

450. BJ II, 55.

451. Ant. XVII, 26-8; XVI, 285.

452. BJ IV, 233-5.

453. Cf. Syria, XLII, 1965, pp. 31-9; Applebaum, The Troopers of Zamaris, Stud. in the Hist. of the Jewish People, Haifa, I, 1970 (Heb.-Eng. résumé), pp. 86, 89.

454. The slogan which is to be found in Mid. Lam. Rab., II, 5 (19) and in Jer. Ta'an. IV, 68-9, attributed to Ben Kosba and also to other commanders (below, p. 60), exhibits an affinity to the activist attitude of the Sicarians. It is: לא תסעד ולא תכסוף which means, literally; "Do not aid and do not desire". As these words are a response to the blessing "The Lord aid you", and as in Mid. Lam. they are addressed to God, and followed by the words: "Thou, O God, hast deserted us and shalt not go forth in our hosts", they are generally interpreted to mean: "Do not aid us, and do not aid our enemies." Cf. the Sicarian attitude - Ant. XVIII, 5; BJ II, 163.

455. B. Lifschitz, BIES XXV, 1961, pp. 72-3.

456. Jer. Ta'an, IV, 8, 68b; Mid. Lam. Rab. II, 2.

457. Y. Devir, <u>Bar Kokhba, the Man and the Messiah</u>, 1964, pp. 25-27.

458. <u>Apol.</u>, I, 31.

459. Eus., <u>Chron.</u> II, p. 168 (Schoene), ad ann. 2149.

460. <u>Chron.</u> II, pp. 168-9 (Schoene), ad ann. 2150.

461. Dindorf, I, 660.

462. IV, 105-106.

463. <u>Op. cit.</u>, II, pp. 41-2.

464. Jer. <u>Ta'an.</u> IV, 68d.

465. Jer. <u>Ta'an.</u> IV, 68a.

466. On coins, Reifenberg, <u>Jew. Coins</u>, nos. 190, 192, 193, 199; in documents: <u>Murabba'at</u>, II, pp. 124-133; <u>IEJ</u> XI, 1961, pp. 41-51.

467. Cf. I <u>Macc.</u> xiii, 42: ἡγουμένου ; xiv; 41-2: ἡγούμενος ; xiv.47: ἐθνάρχης.

468. That various sections regarded Ben Kosba as king, or that some sources name him as such, is not relevant to the constitutional position as defined in the documents.

469. Whether this was a prosecution or a persecution depended entirely on which side of the bar one stood. Technically this was quite a justifiable and legal prosecution within the terms of reference of the Jewish régime. But it does not do to be too technical; there were doubtless religious undertones. As in all cases of a clash between ideologies held as articles of faith, formal prosecution looked like persecution to the accused. The Christians were charged by the Roman authorities with placing Christ above the Emperor; they were accused by the Jewish revolutionary movement, by inference if not technically, of preferring Rome to God.

470. <u>Mid. Lam. Rab.</u>, II, 5 (19).

471. <u>Ibid.</u>

472. 57a.

473. <u>Op. cit.</u>, p. 68.

474. The restriking of extensive issues derived from a wide area by the Jewish insurgents in 132 is the best evidence for the extent and success of their operations before that year. If these coins had not come from over a wide area, they must have been the result of the capture of more than one regimental pay-chest or similar accumulation. The implication in either case would be very similar.

475. Jer. <u>Ta'an.</u> IV, 8, 68b; <u>Mid. Lam. Rab.</u> II, 5 (19); Jer. <u>Ta'an.</u> IV, 68d 68d, 8, 69a.

476. This is nowhere directly attested by ancient sources; the evacuation depends on the acceptance of the evidence of Appian (above, n. 238) and of the much less reliable statement of Eusebius (<u>Dem. Evan.</u> VI, 18,

= PG XXII, 453, ad Zech. 14:2) that Jerusalem was retaken by the Roman forces. Cf. also the inscription discussed here on p. 27.

477. The Scroll of the War of the Sons of Light etc., Yadin, 1957, p. 130 and Yud [6], 15.

478. Op. cit., p. 130, n. 135.

479. H. Van de Weerd, P. Lambrechts, Laureae Aquincenses, I, 1938, pp. 230 sqq.

480. Ibid., pp. 229 sqq.

481. Loc. cit., p. 241.

482. P. Medinger, Rev. arch., 1933, pp. 227 sqq.: L'arc turquois et les archers Parthes à la bataille de Carrhes.

483. L. Lindenschmidt, Tracht und Bewaffnung des römischen Heeres während der Kaiserzeit, 1882, pl. V, 2 and 3. The men represented belonged respectively to the Coh. I Sagittariorum and the Coh. I Ituraeorum.

484. IEJ XI, 1961, p. 20 (Naḥal Tzeelim); Murabba'at, II, fig. 9 and p. 35; BIES XXVI, 1962, p. 153, fig. 7, no. 5; pl. 4, no. 3 (Naḥal David). They are all triangular in section, tanged and equipped with barbs, so resembling those used by the Roman forces. Cf. Brit. Mus. Guide, Greek and Roman Life, 1929, p. 101, fig. 103.

485. I am indebted to Mr. Aryeg Kindler of Museum Ha-Aretz, Tel Aviv, for assistance in obtaining the necessary information on this matter.

486. It should be noted that all the major reverses suffered by Roman imperial forces in the Near East, and some in Europe, in the 1st and 2nd centuries of the current era, were inflicted by heavy mounted cavalry or by mounted archers.

487. Hadrian's well-known letter to Apollonius of Damascus asking for advice on the reduction of ἔθνη καὶ κλίματα ὑπὸ τῆς τυχούσης περιτροπῆς εὐτροπούμενα (Plew, Quellen zur Geschichte Kaisers Hadrian, 1890, pp. 89 sqq.) is shown by Millar (A Study of Cassius Dio, 1964, p. 65) to relate to the Jewish war; Millar has pointed out that the language of Dio's account of the planning of the Temple of Venus and Rome, (LXIX, 4, 1-5) in which Hadrian had committed an irremediable error, (ἀδιόρθωτον ἁμαρτίαν), implies that the Temple was already partly built. As it was inaugurated in April, 121 (Athen., Deipnos. VIII, 361 sq.), this means that Apollonius could have been active as late as 136/7, when the Temple was dedicated. It may of course be remarked that Hadrian would hardly have sent the draft plan to Apollonius when the building was in an advanced state; on the other hand we have Dio's statement (LXVIII, 9, 3) in reference to Dacia, ὁ δὲ Τραιανὸς ὄρη τε τετειχισμένα ἔλαβε which raises the question, why Hadrian should again have needed advice on such conditions in the same country.

Key to Map 1.

Legionary bases	▣
Roman colonies	⊚
Roman military posts before AD 132	◇
" " " after the revolt	☐
Forts garrisoned during the revolt	■
Military units evidenced during the revolt	◆
Jewish centres of dissidence	△

Roads

    Pre-Hadrian ——————

    Hadrian to AD 132 ············

    Hadrian, AD 132-135 —·—·—·—

    "   "   , fortified ══════

    Others — — — —

Forested areas as established by Rost ▨

1.	Kabul Gabri	10.	'Ir Naḥash
2.	Siḥin	11.	Bethlehem
3.	Fiq	12.	Teqoa'
4.	Gamala	13.	Ziph
5.	Beth Yannai	14.	Carmel
6.	Tell Ibrekhtas	15.	Tell Qasileh
7.	Ḥirbet Tzir	16.	Yapha
8.	Antipatris	17.	Migdal
9.	Na'aran	18.	Timna

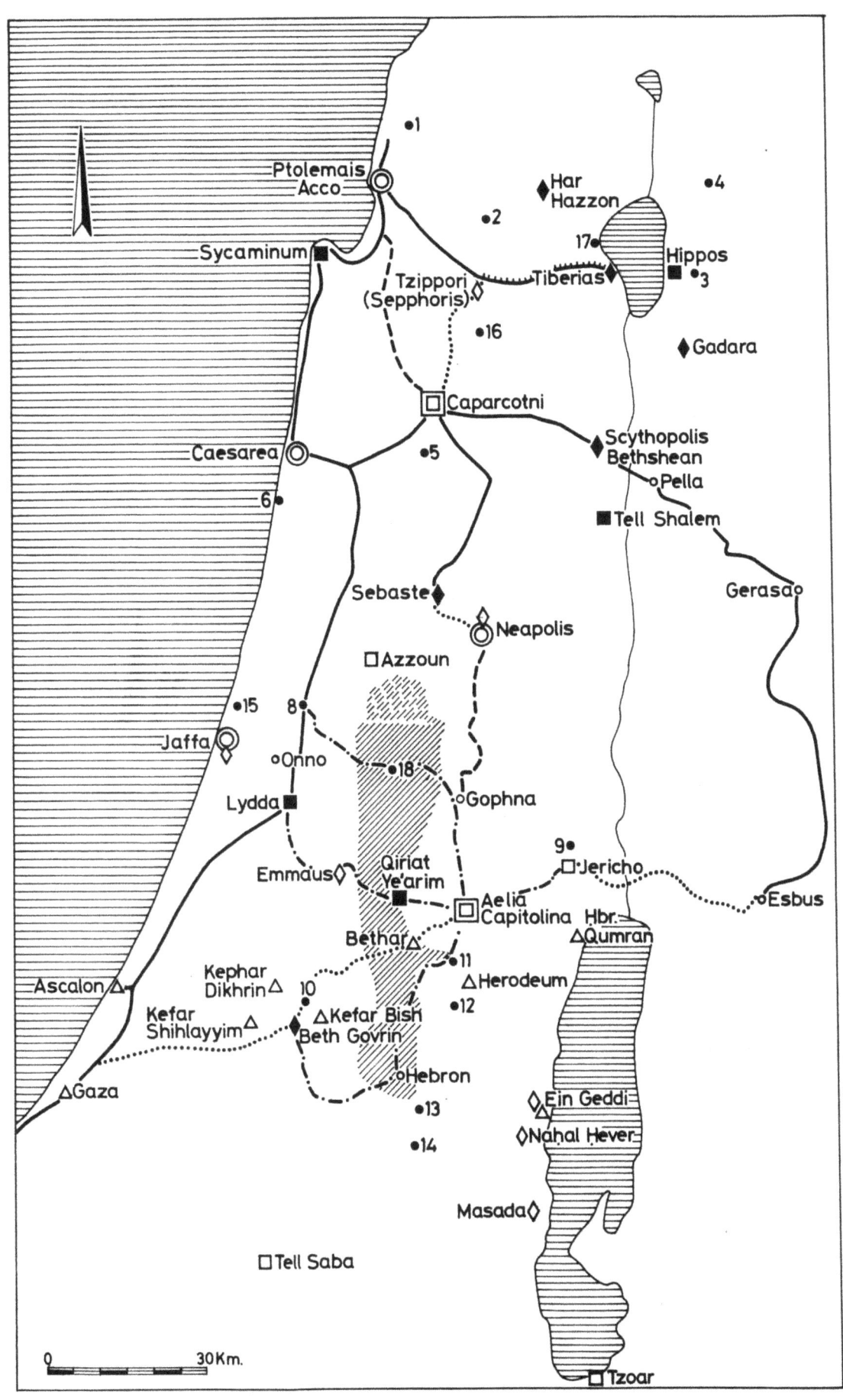

Map 1. Judaea: The localities referred to in the text.

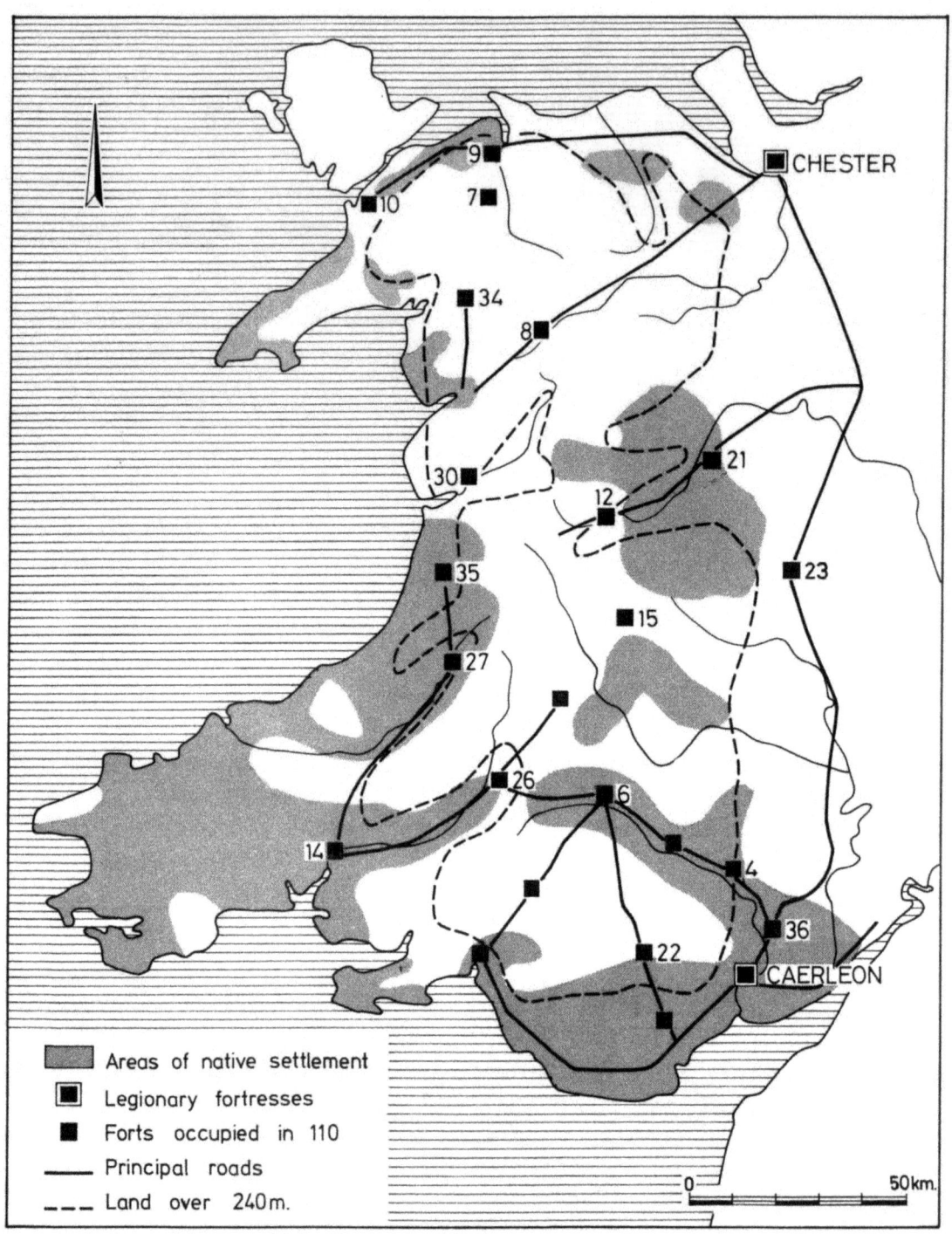

Map 2. Wales: Roman forts held in the year A.D. 110 and their relation to areas of native settlement. (Based on Nash-Williams, Jarrett, <u>The Roman Frontier in Wales</u>, Cardiff, 1969, fig. 5, and various other sources).

www.ingramcontent.com/pod-product-compliance
Lightning Source LLC
Chambersburg PA
CBHW061548010526
44115CB00023B/2980